The Author's Journey

THE
AUTHOR'S JOURNEY

YOUR ROADMAP TO NAVIGATING AND UNDERSTANDING THE PUBLISHING INDUSTRY

MARTINA E. FAULKNER

INSPIREBYTES
OMNI MEDIA

The Author's Journey:
Your Roadmap to Navigating and Understanding the Publishing Industry

Copyright © 2023 by Martina E. Faulkner

This publication is distributed worldwide in the English language in the following formats:

ISBN Paperback: 978-1-953445-39-1
ISBN E-Book: 978-1-953445-40-7

Library of Congress Control Number: 2023939161

This book was responsibly printed using print-on-demand technology in order to minimize its impact on the planet and the environment. Learn more at: www.inspirebytes.com/why-we-publish-differently

▧ INSPIREBYTES OMNI MEDIA
Inspirebytes Omni Media LLC
PO Box 988
Wilmette, IL 60091
For more information, please visit www.inspirebytes.com.

For all the writers and aspiring authors in the world:
Thank you for sharing your voice and your words.

Contents

Introduction

What makes an author and how do we define what it means to be an author? Colloquially, if you ask most people, they associate being an author with a published book. The two keywords being: "published" and "book." In fact, Merriam-Webster defines an author as "the writer of a literary work (such as a book); one that originates or creates something."[1] But being an author is much broader.

Dictionary.com takes it a step further and defines an author as "a person who writes a novel, poem, essay, etc.; the composer of a literary work, as distinguished from a compiler, translator, editor, or copyist."[2] Finally, an even broader interpretation can be found on Wikipedia: "An author is the writer of a book, article, play, or other written work. A broader definition of the word 'author' states: *An author is 'the person who originated or gave existence to*

---

1 Merriam-Webster. (n.d.). Author. In *Merriam-Webster.com dictionary*. Retrieved May 23, 2023, from https://www.merriam-webster.com/dictionary/author

2 Dictionary.com. (n.d.). Author. In *Dictionary.com dictionary*. Retrieved May 23, 2023, from https://www.dictionary.com/browse/author#:~:text=noun,of%20 a%20new%20tax%20plan

anything' and whose authorship determines responsibility for what was created.'"[3]

When we look at the more commonly accepted definition associated with books, there are basically three types of authors:

1. The writer who wants to be validated as a "published author"
2. The writer who wants to share their writing with the world as a career and make money from it
3. The writer who wants to write and hone their craft but doesn't necessarily desire to share it publicly or be published

While there can be overlap, it's better to look at the three types separately so that we can define them and identify the driving force behind an author's actions and decisions. Ultimately, the type of author doesn't guarantee a result. In the world of publishing, there are critically acclaimed works written by published authors who can barely manage to pay their bills. Similarly, there are books that are far from excellent that end up on bestseller lists and make a lot of money. There are also books that are never published that are enjoyed by both the writer and their circle of readers.

In the world of publishing, a "published author" implies that a publishing house has signed your work and therefore invested in you as a writer. Whereas an author is anyone that has written something, as per the Wikipedia definition. In this regard, being an author and being a "published author" are not the same thing, though they are adjacent to each other. This is what gives "published author" a bit more caché in the industry. It's a win. It's something to feel proud of and possibly boast about because someone invested in you.

---

3 Author. (2023, April 29). In *Wikipedia*. https://en.wikipedia.org/wiki/Author

In my own experience, when I have said "I'm an author" when someone asks what I do at a generic event, it is understood that I have written a book. If, however, I am at an industry-related event, the statement usually invites the question: "Oh, with a publishing company, or are you self-published?" In the industry, being a self-published author is often seen as not quite as impressive as being a traditionally published author, even if you are a bestselling author. Do I see this changing in the future? I hope so, but I'm not holding my breath.

As a result, the first type of author (that I am calling the "traditional author") is often more accepted or viewed as being more credible. It could also imply some measure of vanity or ego, but I think it's more than that. The desire to be a "published author" often includes a deep desire to be validated. Or rather, to have your craft, talent, skill, or expertise approved of and celebrated by another entity—one with some influence or power. In this case, that's a publishing company. When a writer gets a contract with a publishing house, it's equivalent to getting a rubber stamp of approval on your work that says,

"You Are Good Enough."

But good enough for what? That's the key question, actually. Is your book good enough to:

- Be a bestseller?
- Line bookshelves in bookstores?
- Teach, inspire, and inform others?
- Make you a public speaker?
- Win awards?
- Sell movie or TV rights?
- Entertain readers?

Unfortunately, the vast majority of work submitted to publishing houses never gets seen. Unsolicited manuscripts can sit in slush piles for years and years. Additionally, there is no requirement for a response. Your manuscript can sit in a pile, and you may never hear from the company. It's a game of numbers. The publishing houses are not at a loss for work to publish, because of the sheer volume of work that is submitted. They hold the upper hand and can pick and choose where to spend their time and money. This is also why it's always best to submit through an agent, if you can. Most publishers won't look at unsolicited work, as it can become a liability if they do. (Top Tip: Always check with a publishing company's solicitation guidelines before you submit anything.)

Let's say your agent gets a deal, or your manuscript makes it out of the slush pile. For a publishing house to take a risk on you and invest in your manuscript, they have to know what the risk is that they are actually taking. Therefore, the question to ask is: What risk factors impact how much investment is being made by the publishing house?

If you're a celebrity, the risk is often minimal, and the "good enough" is more often linked to your follower count than it is to your words, skill, story, or any actual writing (which is why many celebrities work with ghostwriters). As a public figure, your book is often "good enough" if you bring a built-in audience that will create sales.

However, if you're an unknown, the publishing house is taking a chance on their investment. They are publishing something that they *hope* will recoup the financial investment required to bring it to press, but there are no guarantees. Of course, the investment is minimized a bit by the fact that they have in-house teams that they need to keep busy in between other, more successful projects. But it's not risk-free.

This system is not new. This has been the scenario since publishing began—only the players have changed. Now, thankfully, there are more women and more diverse people being offered publishing agreements than there used to be, but that doesn't mean it's equal.

Why has it shifted at all? I believe these changes were made possible by the advent of self-publishing (and subsequently hybrid publishing and vanity publishing), which has forced the traditional publishing industry to shift their approach to choosing what they publish and embrace more diversity, even if it's only a modest amount.

The introduction of self-publishing has also given rise to the second type of author—the "career author." By creating an avenue for authors to be published without the need for approval by a corporate entity, the opportunities to be published have increased dramatically. Now, a savvy writer can become a published author without working with an agent or a publishing house. Of course, there are drawbacks to this. Since there is no bar for acceptance, there is a wide range of professionalism among everything that's self-published. But we will address that in more detail in a later chapter.

So what does this mean for you as a writer or aspiring published author? And what do you want for your writing?

Well, that's what we're going to explore in this book. There are a lot of different ways to become a published author, just as there are different reasons to want to be (or not be) a published author. Understanding these differences and learning what's important to you is what will make your writing career more valuable and rewarding in the long run. It's what will help you create your author's journey.

Let's go!

To begin, this book is deliberately short. Your time is valuable. I respect that. If you're on your author's journey—especially if you're just getting started—it can feel overwhelming, and the plethora of information is not always clear. As such, reading a long(er) book might not be of benefit. Plus, there is so much information online about how to publish that there's no reason to reiterate it here. Therefore, this is not a "how to" book, but more of a "who/what/why" book. This book is designed to bring the main points together in an easily digestible way that's clear and direct in order to help you navigate your journey to becoming—or being—an author.

My goal for this book is to help you understand

1. What type of author you are today (it can change); and
2. What publishing options are currently available.

Once you have a better understanding of these two things, I hope this information will help you navigate your author's journey with more ease and support you in making better decisions for your writing career.

This is a book that can help you understand the publishing industry better, in simpler language. It can also help you learn how the process of publishing can best align with and apply to your unique situation, including your goals and dreams as a writer. Since this is not a "how to" book, if you want to learn *how* to publish your book, I advise you to choose from the numerous options already on the market or hire a professional publishing consultant.

In the subsequent chapters, you will learn how to identify what type of author you are and gain a deeper understanding of the three different types of publishing so you can focus on which one is best for you. You will also be invited to explore how you feel as a writer and whether writing is a career choice or a passion to be nurtured as a hobby (the third type of author).

As of writing this book, I've been a professional writer for over two decades and a publisher for almost ten years. I've watched the industry change and grow in ways I never expected. I've also seen the pitfalls many writers experience on their journeys to becoming an author. Many of these hurdles are avoidable with just a little bit of information and support. Of course, there are always some challenges that come up, but for the most part, the struggle doesn't have to be as difficult or overwhelming as you may think—or as many have reported.

My goal is to share what I have seen and what I know to help you have an easier path. By the end of the book, not only will you know where to focus your efforts, you will also understand why it's important for you to use your resources in different ways. Ultimately, though, my hope is that this book will affirm your passion for writing and be a source of inspiration for you to keep honing your craft and pursuing your dreams, albeit in a more direct and clear way. To that end, I've made an exercise and tips section at the back of the book to help you.

To get started, we first have to identify what type of author you are and why knowing that is important. So let's start there. Here are four questions to ask yourself:

- Why are you a writer?
- What do you love about writing?
- What do you find frustrating about writing?
- What does being an "author" mean to you?

Once you answer these, we can take a deeper dive into each of the author types in the next three chapters.

Author Type 1: The "Traditional Author"

The Type 1 Author is where we're going to start. Borrowing the same distinction I made in the Introduction, this is the author who, above all else, wants to be able to say that they are a "published author" with a traditional publishing house. It may feel a bit vain, and they may also be interested in sales and earning an income from their work. However, most importantly, when asked what they do, they want to answer "I'm an author."

The traditional author is most closely aligned with how the publishing industry has typically worked since its inception. It often follows the same pattern that has always been used, which goes from query letter to agent to book proposal to signed publishing agreement.

This is not to be disparaging about this type of author. We need different types of authors in the publishing industry in order to have as much good work produced as possible. What's important is understanding which type of author *you* are, because knowing this will make your journey easier.

So what might put you in this Type 1 category? Here's a short list of some of the things you might consider:

In general, "traditional authors":

Want to	Do not want to
Be celebrated for their work	Have to do interviews and marketing in order to have their work seen
Be acknowledged for their unique voice and ideas	Maintain a platform to promote their work
Reach and connect with their readers	Have to work on creating avenues or sales to reach their audience
Earn passive income	Rely on sales as their sole income (but often wishes it could be 100% supportive)
Be a "bestselling author"	See their work as a commercial commodity

It may seem like publishing is all about money, and the simple truth is that publishing is a business. As writers, we don't often think of things that way. Our focus is on the craft. But without readers investing their hard-earned income in our work, there is no publishing industry. You can't separate out the business from the creative, though many authors may wish they could.

Historically, that may have been a bit more possible—in fact, it was the primary model of publishing that existed for over a century. But times have changed, and the advent of self-publishing has pushed the industry in ways that the existing system was not set up to support. Today, with the rare exception, publishing is a blend of business and creativity, and that model is here to stay.

As such, the "traditional author" might lean more toward the creative side of things, to the detriment of the business side. There's a reason why Sandra Bullock's character in the 2009 movie *The Proposal* had to get on the phone to convince a celebrated author to do an interview with Oprah. It's known in the industry that (historically speaking) authors were more reclusive and less inclined to engage in sales or anything that promoted their work.

In my career, I have met more authors like this than not. In fact, when my first book *What if..?* came out, and I hired someone to manage a press tour for me, she said to me (paraphrased): "The difference with you is that you're *willing* to do interviews and talk to people. Most authors don't, and that makes it really hard and very frustrating. You make it easier." (Thank you.)

In my opinion, the stereotype of the reclusive author has prevailed for one main reason. In the past, the publishing houses didn't necessarily want the authors to be involved in the business side of publishing. They wanted them to create more material. They wanted them to be good at what they were good at, because that meant the houses could create more and subsequently make more money. The 2006 film *Miss Potter* and the 2019 film *Little Women* somewhat portrayed how the typical relationship between publisher and author has been: You stay on your side, and I will stay on mine. Both films represent the publishing industry of old, but the stereotypes— and expectations—have carried forward to today. Hence, it's often more common for a writer to land in the first type of author category than the second, given what is commonly believed and accepted about the publishing industry.

Again, this is okay, as long as you understand it and know why you are choosing the category you're in. (Yes, it's a choice.) If you're in the first author type, you should probably ensure that you have other means of income as well as other avenues for your craft throughout your writing career. You should also be realistic about your expectations. That is the best way to safeguard yourself against disappointment and frustration. We will address that further in the book. For now, let's focus on what it means to you to be a "published author."

In order to help you explore this further, here are some questions for you to answer. Really dig in here and get honest with yourself. Write your answers, then reflect on them. Knowing the "why" behind your writing is a key element to having success in your writing career.

- What published authors do you look up to? Why?
- What authors do you think poorly of? Why?
- What is your favorite genre to read? Why?
- What genre do you like the least? Why?
- If you had to choose a medium other than writing through which to share your creative ideas, what would it be, and why?
- Who do you want to read your work?
- Would you still write if nobody ever read it? Why or why not?

These questions may seem easy at first, but when you really think about them, they should get you to a place where you feel deeply about what it means to be a writer and why that matters to you.

I remember a meeting I had with two different people early in my publishing career. One was a fellow writer and one was a lawyer I was interviewing to work with my publishing company. Interestingly, the conversations mirrored each other, but each had significantly different perspectives.

When I was talking with the fellow writer, she referenced her science fiction work and suggested that it was on par with (or better than) Suzanne Collins' *The Hunger Games* series and that in her opinion the only reason Suzanne had been successful was because a publishing house had signed her. She went on to say that Suzanne didn't have to do anything but write, and the rest just came to her (the movies, money, etc.). This writer followed it up with: "She's just one author... and anyone can do it." I loved her moxie!

Now, let's contrast that with the meeting I had with the lawyer. She was a creative herself who loved books but chose law to help support other artists, knowing that she didn't want to *be* a creative. As we chatted, I referenced my conversation with the writer and said, "It just takes one book to hit for a publishing house to be viable."

She turned to me, smiled, and said, "And there's *only one* J.K. Rowling. One. In 7 billion." Her perspective was that those "hits" don't come along every day, and are often created with an entire team standing behind them.

Of course, if the writing isn't there, it doesn't matter. As an author, that should be your biggest priority. The writing has to be good, but more importantly, it has to be compelling. Technically correct writing is a requirement. As a reader, there's nothing more frustrating than reading a book you want to love but have to stumble through because of errors and sloppy mistakes. Therefore, a good book also has to be well written *and* have something that captivates the reader. It has to be better than "good."

Both the writer and the lawyer referenced the singular success of a blockbuster book (or, in this case, series). Both saw the potential in such a feat. Where they differed is in the probability. The writer thought, "Anyone can do it," while the lawyer looked at statistics and said, "That's one person in 7 billion."

And that's what really matters here.

You have to know *why* you want to be a published author to know what you're signing up for and what's required of you. You have to know what you're willing to do—or not do—in order to realize your dreams. And, of course, you have to be able to state your dreams. Two different authors in this category might have different goals or dreams. Therefore, understanding *what you actually want* and *why you want it* is what will help you make all the decisions that you're going to have to make as you move through the publishing process.

Now, if you have figured out that you want to be a "traditional author" simply because of what it represents, then that's great. Your focus should be on getting an agent and a contract with a traditional publishing house, regardless of how long it takes. (We will discuss types of publishing houses later in the book, and I will include some discussion about timelines and a brief overview of what is expected from the author.)

I met an author who fit this category a couple years ago. She gave me her book to consider for publishing, and I was willing to option it. She was a first-time author, but unfortunately, she didn't want to do any of the work required to help the book get into readers' hands. She wanted an advance and all the things that typically come to an established and popular author. She hadn't done her research and didn't seem to understand how the publishing industry works. She wanted guaranteed sales and a host of other things. As a new author, I admired her gumption, but was a bit dismayed by the fact that she hadn't conducted at least some basic research into the industry and how things work. Additionally, though her overall story was compelling, there were some serious problems with her manuscript that needed to be addressed.

After we discussed everything, she made it clear that she simply wasn't willing to work beyond her writing. I suggested to her that the best way forward for her was to see if she could find an agent and look for a deal with a bigger house willing to take a risk on an unknown author. I also suggested she do a little more research into the industry itself so that she could engage in conversations and negotiations with a better understanding. I wished her well and genuinely hope she gets a deal. It took our negotiation process for her to realize that she was a Type 1 Author and why that was important for her. From there, she could advocate for her work differently. As a publisher, this was a good example of how not to engage with the publishing industry, especially as a new author. At a minimum, you should research the industry you want to be a part of and gain a clear understanding of how it works. My hope is that this book will do a lot of that for you, though I encourage you to dig even deeper.

Knowing what type of author you are is meant to help you navigate the process with more clarity. If you're not as married to being able to call yourself a "published author" (and all that entails) as much as you are interested in getting your work into the world, earning an income from your writing, and engaging with your readers and audience, then you might be more aligned with the second type of author.

Author Type 2: The "Career Author"

Creatives are storytellers. All creatives. Whether you're an artist, an author, a designer, or anything in between, creatives want to share a story in their work. The wallpaper you choose in your bedroom tells a story. The paint you use on a canvas tells a story. The words you type on the screen tell a story.

Authors are often viewed as storytellers because they work with the written word, but that's just their preferred medium. It's not, however, their exclusive medium. If you are a Type 2 Author, you are probably using multiple mediums to tell your story. From books, to speeches, to podcasts, to social media and so much more, these authors are in this category because they want to engage with their audience. They *want* to share their work in as many ways as possible (that make sense), and they often want to change the world—whether it's through education, inspiration, or entertainment.

The second type of author may still be a "published author," but how they arrive at being published is not limited to working with a traditional publishing house—and wanting others to do most of the work beyond writing the manuscript. In other words, they are open to whatever avenue helps support them in their journey and their craft. Above all, they want to earn a living as an author. They want it to be their career, and they understand that using the word "career" means that they have to blend the business with the creative. As such, this group is probably best described as the "career authors."

This is possibly the biggest shift that has occurred as a result of the recent changes in the publishing industry, brought on mostly by the advent of self-publishing technology. These writers have something to share and will not allow a "rubber stamp" of approval (or lack of thereof) to get in their way. In short, these writers:

Want to	And
Share their work with the world	Understand that they have to be (and want to be) part of the process in doing that
Create and have a platform for their unique voice and work	Manage and engage with the platform to promote their work
Reach their ideal audience and readers	Engage with their audience in meaningful ways on a regular basis
Earn primary income from their work, including their book(s)	Affect change for themselves and positively impact others through their work

This is a different type of author than we have historically seen. They are creative *and* they understand that the world of publishing has changed. They are ready and willing to embrace that change in whatever way they can.

That last phrase matters a lot, so let's say that again: ...in whatever way they can.

This is possibly the most asked question I have received from my authors over the years: *"Do I have to do everything that's out there? Because I don't know how, and I don't want to learn how."*

By "everything," they are referring to the vast array of social media platforms. The short answer is no, of course. But there's a longer, more important answer that aligns with this type of author and helps to empower them to create a rewarding writing career.

On Platforms

Being on every platform is exhausting. Even big companies aren't always on every platform, and they have entire departments and teams dedicated to social media management. Furthermore, if you are on every platform, you're probably not doing it well. Each platform has its own nuance, too. Plus, if you ask any marketing person, they will tell you that the platforms are constantly changing, and they struggle to keep up with the changes... and these are marketing professionals! If they can't keep up, there's no way we can as authors.

What I have told others (and tell you now) is that you should choose the platform that works for you and do it really well. What does "really well" mean, and how should you choose your platform? This all comes back to why you are this type of author, actually.

If you're an author who wants your work to both engage your audience and support you financially, then you will need to engage with your audience, too. In order to do that most effectively, you need to be able to answer these questions:

- What platform does your audience use the most?

- What platform are you most comfortable using, both as an author and as a reader?
- What platform supports the style of engagement you prefer?
- What platform can you commit to being on regularly?
- What platforms talk to each other so you can leverage your content?

These are questions that will make a difference in your engagement. They provide pathways for you to engage with your readers in meaningful ways, which will ultimately lead to sales. As a Type 2 Author, you know that the creative and business need to merge, which means you also know that your engagement should be rewarding for you, intellectually, emotionally, and financially.

It may sound trite, but this type of author is more willing to work for the success of their book. In today's publishing world, a book's success is more dependent on the author than on the publisher. Though it used to be different (which we will discuss in later chapters on publishing), this is how it is today. This type of author understands this and uses this knowledge to help them make the various decisions that arise on the publishing journey.

On Your Why

Your "why" for being published differs from the previous author type in that your focus is more on the long-term journey than on a single book. Your desire to be published stems from your desire to share your creative side in a way that is meaningful and sustaining, whatever that means to you. It's not that you don't have ego or pride wrapped up in being published (or that a Type 1 Author is all about ego or pride). As I already mentioned, your author type is about the driving force behind your work and desire to be published. It's not about the caché, it's about having your work in the world and having an avenue to connect with your readers, often to be able to create more work in the world.

A Type 2 Author doesn't fit the stereotype portrayed in *The Proposal*, as you would *want* to do interviews and show up for your work. Instead of being the reclusive artist creating your masterpiece in a cozy cabin in the woods, you and your work go together. Your books are an extension of you.

Questions to ask yourself:

- How does writing or being an author support your goals as a writer?
- What is most meaningful about writing?
- What do you wish you could let go of in the writing process?
- What does it mean to be an "author" in today's world?
- What authors do you want to emulate? Why?
- Where do you most like to find your next book recommendation?
- How else do you share your creative ideas? Why?
- Who is your ideal reader?
- Would you still write if nobody ever read your work? Why or why not?

Again, there is an overlap between the first two types of authors. Nothing is truly binary or black and white. You may actually fall into each category at different points in your life or career. Or maybe for one book you fall into the second category, but for a different book, you fall into the first. I have experienced that myself. For my first book of poetry, I was more likely to fall in the first category than the second, even though I am most often aligned with the second type of author. Being flexible will help you a long way in your process. Additionally, you can leverage the Type 2 position to sell Type 1 books as part of your career success as an author. There are no hard and fast lines here.

What matters most is knowing what category you are in today—or what category your project falls in—so that you can get clear on publishing your work. Why you want to be published is a question you should be continually asking yourself. As a fellow writer, I can tell you that I still ask myself this question ten years later with almost everything I write. I ask: "Does this need to be published?" or "Why do I want it to be published?" I have numerous pieces of writing (including full-length books) that have yet to be published, and may never be.

Discernment and knowing your "why" will help you as a writer. Identifying your author type will further help you to navigate the world of publishing, which, in turn, should make your writing career more rewarding and sustainable.

That, of course, is if you want to have a career. There are many authors who fall into the third type of author, which we will look at next. These are the "hobbyist authors"—though don't make the mistake of thinking the label "hobbyist" means they aren't professional about their craft.

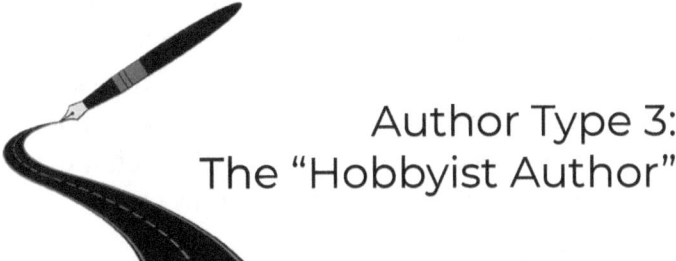

Author Type 3: The "Hobbyist Author"

Thus far, we have focused on the two primary types of authors. These are the authors that are navigating the publishing industry and ultimately want to have their work published and seen by others. The degree of involvement in that process is what shifts them between Type 1 and Type 2 categories. The third type of author—the "hobbyist author"—is different.

These are the authors for whom publishing isn't the ultimate goal. They may still want to share their work with others, and they may get creative about how they do that, but they aren't invested in being a "published author" or using their work for their career. I know a few authors like this, but two in particular come to mind.

In fact, one of them read an early copy of the manuscript for this book and suggested I add this chapter. She was right, of course. To omit this type of author would be a mistake. These authors are diligent, passionate, and incredibly engaged in either the craft of writing, the genre or theme of their work, or both!

To fully understand why it's important to include this type of author, we have to go back to the Wikipedia definition of the word:

"An author is 'the person who originated or gave existence to anything' and whose authorship determines responsibility for what was created."[4]

"Gave existence to anything" is why these professional hobbyists are also authors. Driven by their passion and desire to express themselves creatively, these authors cross all genres, though I'd suggest most are in the fiction, children's, or poetry worlds. (Yes, a poet is an author.) Here are just a few examples of Type 3 Authors and the type of work they're creating:

- Fanfiction serial stories
- Children's books for family
- Family histories
- Online poetry groups (Twitter has an avid community of poets)
- Songwriters
- Short story essayists
- Bloggers (if not for commercial gain)
- Other works of fiction, memoir, or biographies

This group of authors is extensive. Often, you will find entire communities built up around this type of author, either by genre or theme. You may find a lot of "hobbyist authors" in the fanfiction arena. This is partially because most of their work is unpublishable, as it could be a potential infringement of the original author's copyright and/or the publishing company's publishing rights. (This is another area in which it would be good to do some research if you're a fanfiction writer. You don't want to infringe on another author's intellectual property and rights, so make sure you look into what's allowed, or not allowed, in fanfiction.)

Just because the "hobbyist authors" isn't gaining financially from their work does not mean that they are not authors. They are

---

4 Author. (2023, April 29). In Wikipedia. https://en.wikipedia.org/wiki/Author

simply a different type of author, with different goals for their work and a different approach to sharing it with others.

Additionally, some may never share their work with others, and that's okay, too. I have known poets who write for the love of writing who have never shared their work with anyone. In fact, at a recent workshop I gave, I suggested to one of the participants that they consider what will happen to their journals of work after they've gone. It's something we don't often think of as writers, but definitely something we should include in our end-of-life plans. Sorry to get all serious, but it's true. None of us will outlive our writing, and for authors, that's part of the appeal, I think.

Just like the other two types of authors, the Type 3 Author has its own set of statements. Predominantly, the Type 3 Author writes for writing's sake. These writers:

Want to	And
Write	Have no desire to be published
Share their work with a select group of people, or not at all	Don't necessarily want to earn an income from their work
Support their passion	Prefer to keep it as a hobby

When you're an author—when you create something from scratch, from your imagination, experience, or passion—you have a hope that your work will live on. That it will connect with someone, and that it will have a life of its own outside the confines of your mind. Even if you're a hobbyist author, I suspect this is somewhere in there.

One of the things I have told my fellow authors is that you have to know and accept—even embrace—that your work will live forever. This means that it will always be a part of you, and a part of the world. This also means that you have to be willing to support it and talk about it for the rest of your life. We don't get to control when someone finds our work. So it could be 20 years later when someone could be discovering your book for the first time. Being willing to engage with your audience for the rest of your life is part of being a published author. *How* you choose to engage is the variable. Being a hobbyist author does not excuse you from engaging, though it can significantly change how you go about it.

So, are you more of a hobbyist author? In order to help you answer this, here are a few questions to help you reflect.

- Why do you write?
- What are you currently writing?
- How long have you been working on your current writing project?
- Do you write in more than one genre or format?
- Do you like to share your work? Discuss your work with others?
- How would you feel if you never wrote again?
- What other hobbies do you have?

If you are a "hobbyist author," navigating the publishing world may not be as important to you as a Type 1 or 2 Author. That may change for you in the future, just as it may never change. In my experience, almost all of the authors I have ever met have fallen into all three categories at different times in their career—usually based on the scope of their projects. So even if you're a "hobbyist author" today, it would be good for you to understand how publishing works.

Though there only used to be one way to get published (traditional publishing), the options are more varied now. We will look at the different types of publishing next.

Three Main Types of Publishing

Now that we've explored the three different types of authors, it's time to look at the three types of publishing. This chapter is a simple overview of the industry and the three types of publishing that currently exist, along with a couple of personal stories to help you better understand how things have changed and are changing. Today, the three types of publishing are:

- Traditional publishing
- Hybrid publishing (including "vanity publishing")
- Self-publishing

Most people know what traditional publishing is. It is essentially what people think of as "publishing." You submit your manuscript to a publisher (either directly or through an agent) and they choose whether or not to publish it. This model of publishing often involves low royalties and limited input on your part. The more clout you have (or the more popular you are), the more influence you can have on both the process and the royalty rate. Even then, however, your input will probably be minimal, and the publishing house will manage everything throughout the process. Marketing by the publisher will vary based on the book or whether the author is a public figure, though for most authors, it's often minimal. If you're a Type 1 Author, this type of publishing is your dream.

Hybrid publishing has come about in recent years to accommodate the huge volume of work available to publish. In many instances, it's a subsidiary imprint of a traditional publishing house, and can often incorporate the tactic of promising you that the traditional house's editors *might* see your work and therefore offer you a traditional contract. (We're back to the allure and caché of being a Type 1 "traditional author.")

The hybrid model often involves minimal input on your part, which is to your benefit. Why? Because each time you request a change, you're often charged, and those fees can add up quickly. Hybrid publishing is a pay-as-you-go, fee-based model. Even with "package deals," the costs can rise quickly, and the author pays for everything up front. Additionally, the author retains a low percentage of royalties and typically signs over all publishing rights for the work. On the plus side, a professional publisher has created the book, ensuring a good product. This model rarely involves any marketing by the publisher, unless it's paid for by the author.

Self-publishing is exactly what it sounds like. You are the publisher for your work, and you retain everything. You also do everything. The trade-off for doing all the work is keeping all the rewards. Today, we have the technology to make publishing more accessible, which makes it easier to be a published author. As such, the growth of self-publishing in the last decade has been astronomical. It sounds awesome, almost like a no-brainer, but self-publishing has its drawbacks, just like traditional and hybrid publishing.

At the end of the day, only you can know which path is for you. What's important here is understanding what's involved in each one and knowing what you're getting as much as what you're giving up. For example, one of the authors I signed early on in my publishing career reached out to me to re-publish a book she had already self-published a few years earlier. After working with me and my team, she'd realized that her book could have been done more professionally and aligned with her wishes, and she wanted to re-release it. As we got to talking about it, I learned that she hadn't self-published as she thought. Instead, she had used a publishing service that operated as a hybrid publisher. As a result, she no longer had access to her publishing rights. The company charged her for every step of the publishing process (which is what led her to believe she was self-publishing), but they retained the publishing rights as well as 70% of the royalties. This is often the standard. She was understandably upset and had to resign herself to leaving her book with the other company.

It upset me too—which is one of the reasons I am writing this book. Transparency is an undervalued quality in our world, especially in publishing. I imagine that author would have still moved forward with the hybrid company if they had been transparent, simply because she didn't know better at the time. However, knowing differently now, I know she wouldn't sign a contract like that again.

Another aspect of publishing that I feel is undervalued is collaboration. One of the things that I feel strongly about (and why I most often fall in the second category of author) is that I believe collaboration makes a better product. This is not to say that traditional and hybrid publishers don't collaborate with their authors. They do, but the degree of collaboration can vary.

In fact, you can often tell from the acknowledgements in a book whether the author had a close and collaborative working relationship with their editor.

Yes, there's a reason the publisher is the expert, and if you are paying a hybrid publisher for their expertise, you shouldn't have to be chiming in with your opinion and preference. But that's not how the creative process works. If you have a vision for your book cover, for example, it's important that you have a conversation with the designer about it. More importantly, it's important that the collaboration goes both ways. The designer should be able to collaborate with you and share their vision for your book cover after they've consulted with you. Personally, when I explain the "why" behind a book cover's design and what's important to convey, most of my authors respond with, "I never thought of that," and love the result.

Collaboration allows us to think of things we never would have thought of. It creates an environment in which both parties are more equally invested in the end result. As both a publisher and an author, this is the ideal scenario. When you're a writer, you are often investing entire years of your life in your work before it ever hits the shelves. As an author, I would want to know that my publisher is as invested in my book being awesome as I am... and vice versa.

This leads us to another investment-related aspect of publishing that has changed significantly in recent years: the advance.

By now (it's early 2023), we have all heard the stories of the advance that Prince Harry received for *Spare*. Rumored to be around $20 million, it's a hefty price tag for a single book. In order for the publisher to recoup their initial investment (aka: the advance plus the costs of production and their overhead for the book), it's estimated that they will have to sell 1.5-2 million copies of the book, if not more. While the book may eventually do this, it was reported that it definitely didn't on release day as the publisher may have hoped. (Yikes!)

Now, I understand advances. The author in me celebrates when a writer gets rewarded for their work. Historically, creatives have not always been properly compensated for their talent, so advances are one way to ensure some measure of financial success. The problem is that, in recent years, the focus has been too much on the advance. Agents have deliberately created bidding wars for work in order to get as much as they can for their client and themselves up front, since there is no guarantee for anything later.

I get it. Unfortunately, as a publisher *and* as a writer, I don't like it.

In one of the earliest conversations I had with an agent who was negotiating with me for their client, I shared that we don't do advances at our publishing company. I remember him pausing before saying, "You do realize that smacks of not being invested in my client and his work."

I disagreed. "Actually, I think the reverse is true. I think the pendulum has swung too far in the other direction, and these large advances smack of the author and the agent taking the money and running... getting what they can up front so they don't have to invest anything in the work or the promo."

He paused, then said, "I never thought of it that way."

I went on to explain why collaboration is important in publishing. Books live forever. They're one of those investments that are longer than long term. If I'm going to publish an author's work, I want to know that they are as equally invested in their work as I am. I want it to be a relationship, not a one-night stand. The work will live on forever, so the relationship needs to be clearly established and defined from the get-go. What helps to achieve that? Collaboration.

Unfortunately, I don't think collaboration is a driving force behind any of the publishing models. But that doesn't mean that you can't create it. If you're a Type 1 Author, you might not be as interested in collaboration as a Type 2 or Type 3 Author. Therefore, understanding the different types of publishing as well as how you want to engage with your publisher is what will help you make the best decisions you can for your writing career.

So let's start with the model everyone knows but doesn't always understand: traditional publishing.

Traditional Publishing

Traditional publishing is what we all know as "publishing." It's the gold standard for the industry and what most people think of when they think of publishing. Technically, publishing in the Western world started in the mid 1400s with Johannes Gutenberg and his invention of the printing press. (China used block printing as far back as the 9th century, and Korean printmakers used movable metal type about a century before Gutenberg.[5])

Before that, all volumes of work were created by hand, including all words and illustrations. Often, this was done by religious orders, such as monasteries. It's also why most books were owned by the wealthy or the same religious orders that made them. Literacy wasn't a priority for the population.

We, as societies, learned through oral histories. Stories were passed down both within families and communities, and also from our leaders—such as the religious institutions. The printing press is what changed all that. Suddenly, a common person could own a

---

5 Roos, D. (2023, March 27). 7 ways the printing press changed the world. History. https://www.history.com/news/printing-press-renaissance

book and learn to read. Or they could read a pamphlet. Or anything with the written word. The printing press changed the course of history and created the publishing industry. As a result, written words could be marketed... and monetized.

In traditional publishing, an author receives a publishing agreement from a publisher for their manuscript that outlines the details of their arrangement. These details often include, but are not limited to:

- Timeline
- Royalties
- Publishing rights
- Ancillary and subsidiary rights

The specifics can vary from publisher to publisher, or even from imprint to imprint within the same publishing house. For the most part, however, there are "typical" aspects of all traditional publishing agreements. The variability is most impacted by:

1. The material itself (the genre and subject matter, for example), and
2. Who the author is (if they are a celebrity or other public figure).

Other than that, many of the publishing agreements used in traditional publishing are standardized. Things such as the amount of time until the book comes out, final sign-off or approval on proofs or galley copies, as well as termination clauses are all pretty standard within the industry.

In most cases, it's easiest to think of the publishing industry like Vegas: The house always wins. Think about it. If the house didn't mostly "win" in Vegas, it would go out of business. Traditional publishers are no different. They have to "win" in order to stay in business. The blockbuster celebrity memoir helps to pay for the unknown work of fiction on which they are taking a bigger risk. Winning isn't bad, and authors can certainly win in the process, but overall, it's a game of averages and quantity over time. For example, if a publishing house has 1000 books in its catalog and each book earns $100 a month, that translates to approximately $1,080,000 per month for the company (estimated at 90% royalty share). That's not a lot for each book to do, but it keeps the company in business. If it only has 10 books earning the same amount, it will most likely not be in business very long. Publishing is a game of volume and time. The traditional publishing model survives based on volume over time, even if it's a trickle.

In the past, publishers had a lot more sway in getting books into readers' hands. Though there are anti-collusion laws in retail, as a former retail fashion buyer, I can tell you that there are certain aspects of buying that you have little control over. Often, as a buyer, you are limited to what the designer will sell to you. Many people think the fashion buyer gets to dictate most of the transaction, but that's not always the case. If, for example, a premium designer says, "I can give you 100 units," that most likely means that you are allowed to—and possibly *expected* to—buy 100 units of the item. The details will be sorted out later.

Historically, the publishing industry was able to figure out what quantities they would print by working with the various bookstores and roughly establishing (in advance) who would get what. The publisher would then add an overage quantity that would go into a warehouse for future orders. While it was risky, there would be established orders on the books based on relationships the publishers had with their buyers in stores. Since books could only be bought in retail stores, it was a pretty neat and tidy system. Now, as a result of better technology, we can create pre-orders, which helps with this model.

Then along came Amazon.

Amazon started with books. In 1994, Jeff Bezos and his first wife started an online bookstore out of their garage. Books were accessible, relatively inexpensive, used by everyone, and easy to ship. I remember ordering a book from Amazon in those early years and being shocked at how it was shipped. It came with a simple piece of cardboard, shrink-wrapped with a label on top. Minimal packaging, and priced to compete with my local Borders bookstore. Sadly, it wasn't long before Borders went out of business (I still miss it) as Amazon took over.

Today, Amazon's impact on the publishing industry cannot be overstated. They have single-handedly changed the way we buy—and think about—books. Moreover, they have changed the "neat and tidy" relationship between traditional publisher and retailer that I mentioned previously.

As a buyer, I relied on my relationships with vendors to be able to do my job most effectively. It's why I was always able to exceed both my plan and projections, season after season. I knew who to call to get what product to impact my bottom line. I knew when something special was being offered to me, and because I had cultivated good relationships, I was offered a lot of special opportunities. Of course, I couldn't act on all of them, but I was definitely able to make some decisions that were beneficial to the company's bottom line.

Relationships between publisher and retailer are nothing like they once were, and this may be what has had the biggest impact on traditional publishing in recent years. It becomes harder for a publisher to take a risk on an unknown author, and the marketing budgets of 20 years ago have all but gone. Now, it seems, it's more about how big your follower lists are on the various social media platforms than it is about the words on the page. It's also more about how many books you can churn out than it is about the one in front of you.

I have a friend who was in discussions with a major traditional publisher for his first book, which was a nonfiction book about health and well-being. It was a summary text that I think many people would find incredibly informative and helpful. This publisher was interested.

Unfortunately, they wouldn't sign my friend unless he could take the book and turn it into a series of books, with each one focusing on a specific part of the body or aspect of health. They wanted to know that their investment would pay off for a long time to come, or at least be leveraged across a multitude of work, so that they could justify the expense of the marketing they would have to do. Complicated, I know. I wish it weren't that way, but it's not the only time I've heard that same story.

One-hit wonders are not a good bet anymore. Traditional publishers want series and authors who can produce consistently. Think of all the most celebrated authors in recent years—I bet they all have a series or more than one book. The critically acclaimed works are not always the bestsellers.

And that's possibly the most important thing to remember about the traditional houses. They have both the bestsellers *and* the award-winners, and they're not often the same book. In fact, more often than not, the bestsellers are subsidizing the award-winners. Traditional publishing needs the "hits" in order to sign the more thoughtful pieces. If you're a Type 1 Author who has a story to tell, one that leans toward the award category, you're going to need a traditional house that is willing and able to invest in your work.

Personally, I still believe in traditional publishers as the gold standard for publishing because they hold the bar (for the most part) on quality of work. As you will learn in the next two chapters, hybrid publishers and self-publishing have lowered the bar for what's deemed "good work" in the world. It's a shame, in my opinion, because it's something that affects all of us who love this industry.

While traditional publishing isn't perfect and there is a lot that could change for the better, there is one area that I *really* think needs to change: There should be more room for competition in the industry. Thankfully, a recent merger attempt between two of the biggest publishers (Penguin Random House and Simon & Schuster) was shot down in late 2022. This merger would have taken the "Big 5" to the "Big 4" and would have created a mega publishing house—one that no other publisher could compete with.[6]

Competition in publishing is good for all parties involved. More options can only benefit the industry as a whole because it would allow for more varied work to be brought forward. As competition decreases, so do opportunities for new writers. While you may think there are a lot of publishing houses in the world, the truth is that there are a lot of *imprints*, not houses.

I remember when I began my own publishing journey, I started doing a lot of research into the industry. I was shocked to find a timeline on Penguin Random House's website that showed just how the company had slowly acquired most of the publishing houses I thought were independent. While I'm all for leveraging

6 The Associated Press. (2022, November 1). Judge blocks Penguin Random House-Simon & Schuster merger. NPR. https://www.npr.org/2022/11/01/1133032238/judge-blocks-penguin-random-house-simon-schuster-merger

resources (especially in light of climate change and the damage we've done to the planet), it's pretty surprising to see. Starting in 1838 with G.P Putnam's Sons, Penguin Random House now has over 300 imprints and brands operating in 20 countries.[7] Their entire history is represented visually in an incredible timeline on their site that's worth checking out as well.[8]

Ultimately, the decision to publish with a traditional publishing house is yours to make, and while you can certainly choose it, unfortunately, there is no guarantee that a publishing house will sign your book. These days, without an agent, it's unlikely you would get in the door. Even with an agent, it can still be difficult, though not impossible. It all depends on the work that's being submitted. Publishing houses often seek specific themes or genres based on the gaps in their current catalog or what they see selling well, and agents will know this. If you do your research, you stand a much greater chance of being signed by an agent and getting a publishing deal than if you blindly submit.

Agents are the primary pathway to traditional publishing that allow the Type 1 author to achieve their dreams and be able to say they are a "published author." Knowing this desire among authors exists, the publishing industry has learned to capitalize on it by creating the hybrid publishing model, which we will look at in the next chapter.

The hybrid publishing model allows authors who otherwise didn't get a contract to be published professionally by a company. It's a model that gives authors a path to publishing where the publishing company does not have to incur financial risk, though

---

7 Penguin Random House. (n.d.). Our story. https://www.penguinrandomhouse. com/about-us/our-story/

8 Penguin Random House. (n.d.). Company history. https://global.penguinrandomhouse.com/company-history/

they still receive a financial reward. Beyond that, it allows the publishing house to accept a broader amount of work and build their catalog. Remember, publishing is a numbers game. The more books you have in your catalog, the more stability you have as a publishing company. Hybrid publishing can be a good option for the Type 2 Author who wants to be published and doesn't want to do all the work, provided the details of the contract are clear from the start.

Hybrid Publishing

Hybrid publishing is sort of a combination of traditional publishing and self-publishing. Sort of. As such, in hybrid publishing, you are both the client and the talent, but that doesn't necessarily mean you are the one in charge. Does that make sense? Probably not. It didn't to me, either.

I received a publishing offer with my first book from a hybrid publisher with a "dangling carrot" of getting my work in front of the main (traditional) publishing house that owned the hybrid. It's a story I share often and the reason I got into publishing.

With my first book, I sent the manuscript out to beta readers and received incredibly positive feedback. In fact, one of my readers shared it with a former colleague who had retired from publishing as a senior editor. Her feedback was very clear. It wasn't a matter of *if* I would get a contract, it was a matter of *when*. I remember feeling a bit shocked at the time, and I wasn't sure what I needed to do in order to change the "if" to the "when." Unfortunately, this individual was retired, and people in publishing have a tendency to protect their resources. Other authors I knew at the time also made similar commitments to their agents to not share their information. It's standard practice. So if someone isn't sharing that information with you, don't take it personally.

Ultimately, I did get a referral to a major house. Since I didn't have a name or a significant following, I was told that while they were interested, they couldn't take the risk. Instead, they offered for me to work with their hybrid imprint. Then, if the book did well, they would possibly invite me into the main publishing house.

I received the 20+ page contract from the hybrid house and read it one paragraph at a time. I made copious notes. My father was a lawyer, so I was doing my best to get really clear on everything. In the end, I remember feeling deflated. I sent the contract to a friend in New York who had worked in the magazine industry. I asked her two simple questions:

1. Is this contract typical/standard?
2. Would you sign it?

Her answers were clear: Yes. And no.

It was a typical contract, with all the standard terms and conditions found in publishing agreements, and she wouldn't sign it. She then went on to ask me why I wasn't considering self-publishing instead. In her mind, the contract made it clear that I was going to have to do almost everything myself or pay them a lot to do it, so why not keep the rights and the royalties? She had a point.

I went back to the hybrid house and asked a lot of questions. In the end, the relationship soured because I pushed back on the agreement, and I ended up having to speak with a manager about the representative's aggressive language and behavior toward me. It was incredibly unpleasant. It was only a few years later that I realized the reason why. It was sales. The "editorial representative" was actually in sales. She wasn't an editor or a publisher. Her job was to get me to sign the agreement, guaranteeing the company many thousands of dollars. It all felt horrible.

At the time, hybrid publishing wasn't for me. But that doesn't mean it can't be for you. The most important thing is to ask a lot of questions and get very clear on the details. The easiest way to look at hybrid publishing is as a fee-for-service model and understand that there are both up-front fees and other fees at the back end (in the way of keeping royalties and rights). For an established, up-front fee, you will receive a specific package of services. Every hybrid publisher I have seen has publishing packages that range in price, and many have à la carte services as well. While all of the various services are listed in the package, the devil is in the details—or in this case, the fine print.

For example, if editing is included in your package price, the question to ask is how many editing passes there are. How many times can you go back and forth with your editor? Are you assigned one editor, or a group of editors? Some packages limit the number of editing passes to three, which, in my experience, is rarely enough. If you are limited and you go beyond the included number, how much are you paying thereafter? All of these things matter because they can add up very quickly. Editing takes time, and an editor should be compensated for their work. The issue is not the cost of the editing, it's making sure you know the details before you sign on the dotted line.

When you understand that it's a fee-for-service model, then you can ask the right questions. You can also choose what services you want, such as: editing, design, marketing, etc. Each service is a different step in the publishing process and is required if you want your book to look professional. But, if you have a good editor yourself, you may want to skip that step with the hybrid publisher. Or if your book cover has already been designed elsewhere, you can probably bring that to the table and negotiate to remove that fee from the contract.

A hybrid publisher can do almost everything a traditional publisher does, they just charge you for it in advance while still keeping a large percentage of the royalties. Most hybrid publishing contracts I've seen put the rate at 70% to the hybrid publisher and 30% to the author. Though I believe we are starting to see this change as more and more authors become savvy and negotiate better. Plus, there are more hybrid publishers in the industry now, and some are creating more author-friendly models. They're still using the fee-for-service approach, but they are adjusting some of the details to be more equitable, financially. Be a savvy consumer and do some research to get the best deal for yourself.

One of the things that is rarely adjusted in the hybrid contract is the publishing rights. As of today, most hybrid publishers (and all traditional publishers) retain the publishing rights for your work. I say "most" because I've recently heard about at least a few hybrid publishers not keeping the publishing rights, but they might be vanity presses instead that typically accepts any work. Assigning the publishing rights means that you can't offer your book to any other publisher or company without the original publisher involved in the negotiations, including overseas translations. Publishing rights often include ancillary and derivative rights, too. These are things like TV or movie rights and merchandising rights. It can also include rights to converting the material to online learning portals. This protects the publisher from having another company benefit from their work and expertise. In many ways, it also protects you as the author, as your copyright is more easily defended by a publishing house instead of by you alone. The only downside to this scenario is that you can't just go somewhere else if you're unhappy with your publisher. You'd have to negotiate and buy back your publishing rights to do that. This can be costly if you're a successful author, though I know people who have done it.

A hybrid publisher can be a very good option for an author who develops work on a regular basis and has been unsuccessful in getting a traditional publishing contract or agent but doesn't have the time or expertise to handle all the various steps involved in self-publishing. It can also be a very good option for a one-time author who wants to be published but doesn't know where to begin and wants the process to be easy. Of course, with hybrid publishing, you need the resources to pay for the services. So that will factor into your decision.

To decide whether a hybrid model is good for you, ask yourself these questions:

- What am I willing to spend to get my book published?
- What am I willing to give up, and what do I want to retain?
- How quickly do I want to be published? (Since hybrid publishing is paid for by you, it's often much faster than traditional publishing, and since they do the heavy lifting for a fee, it can be faster than doing it yourself.)
- What services do I really want to pay for, and what am I willing to do myself?

By answering these questions, you will be better able to make your decision between hybrid publishing and pursuing a traditional publishing agreement. Remember, a traditional publishing house will not charge you for any services they provide as part of the publishing deal, and a hybrid publisher will. While there might now be a few exceptions in the hybrid world, both will keep the publishing rights and both will keep the majority of the royalties, and neither publishing model can guarantee you sales.

It also bears noting that not all hybrid publishers accept all work. Many hybrid publishers behave more like traditional publishers, and require the work to meet a certain level of quality or interest. Meaning, the work has to be both good and interesting enough to fill a space in the market. Even though you are paying to be published, the publisher's name is still on the book, and they have a reputation in the industry to uphold. As such, they don't accept everything that crosses their desk. It's not a publishing service that anyone can access.

There is, however, a sub-category of hybrid publisher that does accept anything and everything. This is most often referred to as a "vanity press." A vanity press is a publisher for hire. Meaning, if you're willing to pay the fee, they will provide the service, often without regard to the quality of the work. If you've spent any time in writer's groups online, you know there are a lot of mixed feelings about vanity presses. From where I stand, they have both good and less-good aspects.

Years ago, in one of these writing groups, I once saw a book a man had written with his recommendations for fishing in a single lake or river in Minnesota. It was such a specific topic with such a limited audience that it was no wonder it wasn't accepted by traditional or hybrid publishers. He didn't want to have to do everything himself, and he had the resources to pay the vanity press, so it was a good solution for him.

With over 1 million books published each year, there are many routes to being published. Of course, these aren't the only options available to you, so let's shift gears and look at self-publishing.

Self-Publishing

Self-publishing is pretty direct and self-explanatory. You are publishing your book yourself and doing all the things a publisher would do. Ideally. As such, I'm going to break this chapter into two segments:

1. What you absolutely must do to self-publish professionally and be taken seriously as an author
2. How you can leverage experts to make self-publishing easier

Let's start by discussing how this third type of publishing came about. If you have a love-hate relationship with Amazon, this chapter might only serve to reinforce it. However, as a writer, my guess is that you might end up loving Amazon a little bit more after reading this, even if you think of them as a necessary evil. So let's start there. In short, Amazon is the main reason the publishing industry is changing. We're still deep in the change, and though it's unclear where we will end up, my hope is it will be much better.

As we've already discussed, Amazon started as an online bookstore. Historically, books were at the core of what Amazon did.

While they have expanded (significantly) beyond books, and most of their income is no longer from books (seriously, their web services division is massive), it seems that books will always be part of Amazon's business model. Thankfully.

I say thankfully because their role in the publishing industry is what has made self-publishing at scale possible. This means that you can self-publish to a wide audience without having to print, warehouse, and ship vast quantities of your book yourself. Your reach can be global without you having to create a global business or subcontract with other businesses. The Amazon platform has opened up publishing to an entire group of authors—for better and worse.

The good news is that anyone can publish on Amazon.

The bad news is that *anyone* can publish on Amazon... and they do.

This is where understanding what makes a book look and feel professional matters. If you're going to self-publish, it's time to roll up your sleeves and make some lists.

Self-Publishing as a Professional Endeavor

When I self-published my first book, I decided to take the time to learn what traditional publishing houses did and mimic them. I learned about editing, design, and marketing, among many other "smaller" and more nuanced publishing-related elements. But editing, design, and marketing are the big three. They are the things that you absolutely need to include in self-publishing your work if you want to be taken seriously as an author. Since you are working with intellectual property, you will also want to understand the legal specifics, which I will highlight in a bit.

At the time, I remember being acquaintances with another author on Facebook who had just self-published his book. He created a private group of friends/supporters and asked if anyone was interested in reading his recently published e-book for free in exchange for writing a review. This is a fairly common practice, and a good way to get reviews. I volunteered.

The book was good. It was a work of fiction, and the story was compelling and well thought out. The main character was a bit flat at times and somewhat contrived, but overall, it was a decent work of fiction. However, it hadn't been properly edited.

This author didn't make the choice to pay a professional editor to look at his work. He thought he was a good writer and published his book without professional help. The book was riddled with typos and grammatical errors. At times, it made it difficult to read. I gave his book 4 stars, and he got upset with me. He reached out to ask me why I didn't give him 5 stars, since we were friends. (I guess it was assumed that I would give him 5 stars based solely on our acquaintanceship or the fact that I received the book for free.)

I explained to him that I would have given it 5 stars if it had been edited, but that the numerous errors detracted from the work. He remained upset and sent me an unkind message and ended our acquaintance.

Now, we all make mistakes (#tpyoshappen). See what I did there? We *all* have typos. I still make typos when I write. However, every writer on the planet will tell you that their work is better for having been edited. And yes, even editors miss things. But to not even invest in professional editing in the first place is a mistake too many self-published authors make, and it's partially why self-published authors get a bad rap. The other reason is design.

Book design is completely unique. We are talking about the interior here. The actual words on the page. Yes, you can download a template from Amazon's KDP (Kindle Direct Publishing) or use another software provider, but a professional designer goes beyond simply loading words onto a template. They look at the spacing between letters (called "kerning") and adjust where necessary. They break words appropriately from one line to another, and they prevent "widows" and "orphans"—which are lines of text that dangle either at the beginning or the end of a block.

Book designers are typesetters in the same way that typesetting has been done since the advent of the printing press. If you think back to the printing press and even old typewriters, each letter was produced by putting ink on a metal stamp and then "pressing" them onto paper to form words. A typesetter was the person who placed all the stamps in a row to make the sentences. It was a highly skilled occupation, though I'm not sure it was well compensated.

In my opinion, book designers are incredibly valuable, as a well-designed book is easier to read. Plus, the designers stay on top of the shifting "standards" in the publishing industry, as well as where or how you can be more creative with design and use things like pull quotes to highlight a phrase or thought. Unfortunately, book design is another area that self-published authors often skip, believing that they can just use a word-processing program online. Now, if you're only publishing in e-book form, perhaps that's true. But if you want a hard copy of your book (paperback or hardcover), you should use a book designer.

Investing in editing and interior design will make your self-published book more professional. However, cover design is possibly the most overlooked aspect of self-publishing that can instantly tell a reader your book is not professional. Book cover design is incredibly unique in the graphic design world and requires both experience and expertise. I often tell my authors that it is the *most* limited real estate to effectively and compellingly tell a story in only a glance.

Think about it, every book cover has the same two required elements: title and author. Beyond that, you may also have:

- A subtitle
- A blurb or endorsement
- Graphic images
- Artwork
- The publisher's logo (though this is typically on the spine and back cover)
- Awards or achievements

Book cover design is virtually infinite in how you can combine all these elements to tell a story. Get it wrong, and your book won't attract an audience. Get it right, and your audience can expand exponentially. Unfortunately, a lot of self-published authors think the cover doesn't matter as much as the interior. While that may be true on some level, without a good cover, nobody is going to get to the interior. There's a reason we have the saying "Don't judge a book by its cover," because we all do!

It bears noting that the cover also includes the spine and the back. It's important to be incredibly purposeful about all three aspects of the cover because this is how most people "shop" for books. If you're in a bookstore, the vast majority of the books on the shelf are displayed by the spine. If you make the spine an after-thought, you're missing out on an opportunity to gain interest in your book. Similarly, the right description, blurb, and author bio (and photo) on the back cover can mean the difference between someone buying your book or putting it back on the shelf. This is why authors are authors and designers are designers. An author *should* be more focused on the words inside the book and hire an expert to help them convey the story on the cover.

This is why I say that "the bad news is that *anyone* can publish on Amazon." Poorly written and poorly (or non-) edited books can be published on Amazon. Poorly designed books can be published on Amazon. Literally anyone can publish their work on Amazon. So how do you set yourself apart from everyone else? Invest in your work. Treat yourself to the same level of expertise and professionalism that a publisher would provide. You deserve it, and your work deserves it. And if you don't know where to begin, there are many individuals with the expertise you need that can help.

Leveraging Experts to Self-Publish Professionally

Just as hybrid publishers and vanity presses have grown in recent years, so have experts in publishing. Many of them are former publishing professionals who spent years at a traditional publishing house and wanted a lifestyle change. In order to use their expertise and continue in a field they love, they became publishing consultants. These are professionals who range from editors to designers to marketers and publicists. They cover the spectrum of services you might want to hire to help you navigate the process while remaining self-published.

This begs the question: Why would you want to do this instead of going with a hybrid publisher? The answer is simple, because even though you are still paying for all the services, with self-publishing you retain all of the rights and royalties. It will be much more work, but the reward can be exponentially greater. It will also teach you how to publish, which you can then use for a future book.

In my experience, these professionals run the gamut, just like almost any other industry. There are some that you probably wouldn't want to work with, and there are some that you would have to mortgage your house to work with. My suggestion is to aim for something in the middle and always go by referral. The best consultant is one that has worked with and/or been recommended by someone you know. Once you have a recommendation, you need to figure out what it is you actually need help with. When we look at the three main aspects of publishing—editing, design and marketing—the one we haven't addressed yet is marketing.

To many authors, marketing can feel like a bad word. It can also feel incredibly overwhelming. I think that's because we think of marketing as advertising and instantly imagine *Mad Men* and all the smarmy antics of the advertising industry. But nothing could be further from the truth. Marketing, as an author, is about connection. It's about identifying your audience and connecting with them. Engaging with them. Why wouldn't you want to do that?

Hiring a marketing professional will help you figure out what to do and when, but ultimately there is an important truth to remember: People buy books from other people. They don't buy books from companies, such as publishers. They buy books because they a) already like the author and their work, b) their friend or family member recommended the book, or c) their local or favorite retailer suggested the book. People buy books from other people. When you understand this and truly accept it, you can turn marketing into an opportunity to connect with your audience in a new way.

Of course, it can be a lot to manage a good marketing plan, and that's where a publishing expert can help. Though they can't participate in a podcast for you, they can help you set up a podcast tour and manage your calendar. They can also help you design graphics for your social media as well as develop a promo calendar that retains your authenticity.

Leveraging experts to help you self-publish is about understanding what's needed, assessing what you are able to do on your own, and identifying where it makes sense to use your resources to hire someone else. There's one area, however, where I think it is important to hire a professional: legal issues.

If you are self-publishing, please don't overlook the legal aspects of publishing. I have provided more information in the next chapter, but this subject is important enough to state twice. At a minimum, this includes registering your work with the Library of Congress (if you're in the United States) and legally copyrighting your book. Registering your book with the Library of Congress is free and only requires you to set up an account with them (more information on this in the resources section at the back of the book). To register the copyright for your work, you have to pay a fee and fill out a form online. This is where it matters to hire someone. Though you can probably teach yourself what to do, it's much better to hire someone who knows what they're doing. In the end, you will save yourself money and headaches if the copyright is done correctly from the start. This is your work—please protect it. There are professionals available to help you do just that.

Why It's Important to Invest in Yourself as an Author

In the end, it's about investing in yourself as an author. If you're reading this book, my guess is that you want to be taken seriously as an author, and the best way to do that is to invest in your work. As a self-published author, if you're not willing to invest in your work and publish it professionally, it begs the question: Why are you publishing at all?

Too many self-published authors have not invested in their work. As a result, there are a lot of bad books online. If you're self-publishing solely to be able to call yourself an "author," the least you can do is honor the craft and the industry and do it as professionally as you are able. If funds or resources are limited, use them wisely.

If, however, you're self-publishing in order to share your work with the world in new and/or more meaningful ways, then you owe it to your work (and yourself) to do it as professionally as possible.

At one point in my writing career, I had joined a writing group online. It was a consortium of various writers, all of whom were planning to be or already were self-published. One of the members asked if anyone would be willing to read three chapters of her work and provide feedback. Again, I volunteered, along with four other people. The writer asked us to share our feedback publicly in the group on a thread she had created. (I actually think she assumed the feedback would all be favorable and would subsequently create interest in her work.)

Unfortunately, the three chapters were not good. The storyline was drawn from an existing (and significant) work that was already a movie, and she hadn't edited the chapters at all. In addition to typos, spelling mistakes, and poorly crafted sentences, there were actual passages that one of the other volunteer readers said were pulled directly from the original work. The writer fought back and said it was all her own work and that she had had the idea *before* the author of the existing work, which was already a few years old. In the end, she did herself more harm than good by inviting others into her work without first investing in it. Aside from the overlap with an existing work (which is a major issue itself), it wasn't edited at all. However compelling, an unedited story is not enough to make a good book... or a book worthy of publishing.

I believe that there are many people who think that they will be the next *Harry Potter* when they self-publish. Their story is exciting or compelling, and they feel certain that if people would "just pick it up" they'd have massive success. But the simple truth is that even in the publishing world with all the resources and expertise of a traditional publishing house, *Harry Potter* was an anomaly. If it had been self-published, who knows if it would have gone much beyond the first book.

What we do know, however, is that self-publishing has been a gift to the publishing world. Not only has it allowed writers who otherwise would not have been published to get their work into the world, it has forced the publishing industry to change and evolve. The industry is still in the process of evolving, and I think it always will be as technology changes—which is a good thing. Self-publishing has forced a fairly antiquated system to reinvent itself, for better and for worse.

As a writer myself, I think that self-publishing has forever changed the publishing landscape for the better. Yes, even with the amount of unedited and poorly designed books now for sale online. If you're a writer who longs to share your work with the world, even if "the world" is only your friends and family, you can now do so relatively easily and inexpensively thanks to self-publishing. And, as the technology continues to evolve and improve, it will only get easier.

The downsides, of course, are often financial. I have seen a lot of pushback on the price for books of late. In truth, the retail prices for books have not kept pace with the rest of the retail world. Books are *much* less expensive than they ought to be, considering inflation and the increases in the cost of living. But the volume of books produced each year and the stiff competition to make it onto readers' shelves has definitely helped keep the prices down. Perhaps that is the most significant downside to self-publishing when it comes to the industry as a whole.

For authors, the main downside is the financial investment they *should* make in order to publish their book most professionally. You may be surprised to know that it costs, on average, $3,000-5,000 to properly publish a book, and it can often go much higher depending on what's involved. In order to assess if self-publishing is right for you, the key questions you need to ask yourself are:

- Why do you want to be published?
- What is the desired outcome you want to achieve with your book?
- What is your budget to bring your book to life?
- How much work are you willing to do?

Self-publishing can be a lot to take on, but the rewards can also be well worth it. It's an investment in your work that is both significant and, at times, overwhelming. In self-publishing, you own 100% of the rights and royalties, as well as 100% of the work (other than what you can outsource, though you're still the manager). Of course, there are many ways to achieve the end results you desire with help from others, but the first step is knowing that you're willing to invest in yourself and your work in this way. Beyond that, anything is possible.

Where, When, and How to Invest in Being an Author

Now that we've explored the different types of authors and publishing, there are some smaller details to look at when it comes to being an author. While some of these things will only apply if you choose to self-publish, they are all good things to know about in the publishing industry.

After working directly with authors for over five years and being in the publishing industry for almost ten, I have found that most authors don't know about most of the basics of publishing. As I said in the previous chapter, based on area of expertise alone, it would be great if authors could focus on the writing and leave the other stuff to the experts. Unfortunately, that's rarely how it works these days, and you really should have a working knowledge of publishing, even if you're outsourcing everything. This will help you navigate the process with more ease and confidence. Before we get into the details, though, one simple bit of advice for anyone who is considering signing a publishing contract with a traditional or a hybrid publishing company: If you can, please hire a lawyer to review any contracts before you sign. You will be glad you did.

Now, let's revisit some of the more "legal" aspects of publishing.[9] Most of the authors I have worked with were unaware of what needs to happen in order to protect your work. In short, everything you create falls under the category of "intellectual property." This is why plagiarism is such a big deal, even though I've heard more than a few people dismiss it by saying, "What's the big deal? It's just words." To take someone else's intellectual property and pass it off as your own is stealing. Plain and simple. You wouldn't go into someone's house and steal their armchair or their jewelry, would you? No. Property is property. I've been a victim of having my intellectual property stolen, and I know plenty of other creatives who have as well. Here's a simple warning that I hope you take to heart: Just because you find something on the internet doesn't always mean you're allowed to use it in your work. In other words, if you don't know if you should cite the work, you probably should. You would want the same done for you.

Of course, it's easy to prove deliberate theft of the written word when it's published somewhere, especially if you can link it back to something you've already created that you know was received by the person stealing it. But it's harder when it's done unintentionally, like when you use somebody else's photo to create a meme without the photographer's approval. This is why sites like Unsplash are a great resource for creatives. (What is Unsplash? It's an online site for open-source photography that you can use for any project.) This is also why I always advocate for giving credit where credit is due. If you like someone's words, quote them. If you like a photo, ask if you can use it if you give credit. Even if you use something like Unsplash, it's always a good practice to make mention of the photographer somewhere. As creatives, we are all on the same

---

9 Disclaimer: I am not a lawyer, and this segment does not serve as legal advice. It is a reference section only and does not replace actual legal advice from a professional.

team. A good practice is to treat other creatives the way you would want to be treated.

Personally, when I found that something I had written was used in someone else's writing—without credit—I chose to act and confront the person directly. I did so without emotion by simply sharing that I had noticed that they used it and asked them to send another message indicating that it was, in fact, someone else's idea and words. In the case where I had a meme taken from me and shared on social media, I simply commented on the post saying, "Thank you for sharing my graphic. I can't believe it's been six years since I created this. If you want to see the original post, click here." This way, the individual in question *and* all their followers would see that it was someone else's work. This is also why I now add the copyright symbol (©) and my name to everything I create, at a minimum. To make it clearer, I also put it somewhere in the middle of the words or design so that it can't be cropped out. Wherever possible, I will also add the year and the phrase "all rights reserved" as that's the best way to do it.

Confronting people who take your work, whether intentionally or not, may or may not be something you want to do. Personally, I think it's always a good idea to assess whether it was done with intention, as it's often not. But, most importantly, knowing your options and having legal representation is key to understanding what you can and cannot do when it comes to intellectual property. This is also why it's important to legally copyright your book by obtaining a copyright registration. A lot of self-published authors skip this step, thinking that just adding the © on the copyright page is enough. Sort of, but not really.

As an author, you are the owner of all copyright interest in your work as soon as it is written. However, registering the copyright with the copyright office gives you additional legal protections that you wouldn't have otherwise. Obtaining a copyright registration for your book is proof that you are claiming this work as your own, and it gives you more power to go after anyone who infringes on your copyright. This includes 1) having the ability to file a lawsuit to stop infringement and 2) being able to obtain some damages that are only available with a registered work.

On more than one occasion, I have been grateful to have the legal filing for both my own work and my authors' work. There is a set fee (currently $65) associated with filing a legal copyright as well as a limited timeframe in which to complete the process. The process isn't the easiest, but it's 100% worth it. Traditional publishers do this for you, and I assume hybrid publishers do as well. If you are self-publishing, you can also often find consultants that offer this service if you find it daunting. (You don't want to get it wrong.)

Other legal- or professional-related aspects of publishing that you will want to consider include:

- ISBN registration
- LCCN registration
- Trademark (for specific phrases, for example)
- URL or unique website (for you as an author, your book, or both)
- Joining a professional group, such as the Authors Guild

The ISBN (International Standard Book Number) is a unique 13-digit number that identifies your book or book-product. Each format of your book needs to have its own ISBN. This means that if you publish your book in three formats (paperback, e-book, hardcover), you need a separate ISBN for each. The place to get your ISBN is through Bowker Identifier Services (myidentifiers. com). You can purchase them in bulk or one at a time. If you are publishing through a traditional or hybrid publisher, they do this for you. If you are self-publishing, you will want to do this yourself. Getting an ISBN varies in price based on how many you are purchasing at one time. If you know you will self-publish more than one book, it would be cheaper to buy a set of ISBNs than buying one at a time. Amazon offers assigned ISBNs for your work for free, but it's unique to them and cannot be used elsewhere. This means your book cannot be published elsewhere using the Amazon ISBN, making it unavailable to other retailers, libraries, and bookstores. Ultimately, it's more professional to own your ISBNs.

Registering your book with the Library of Congress (in the USA) in advance of its release is what creates the LCCN (Library of Congress Control Number). This is the identification number assigned by the Library of Congress for all of the books in its cataloged collections. While this isn't a legally required step, it *is* the more professional way to go. Again, a traditional and hybrid publisher should be doing this for you. It's free to register your LCCN, whereas a copyright registration carries a fee, as I've already mentioned.

Sometimes you may write something that is so important that you might want to trademark it. This is definitely more rare, but it can happen, especially in the nonfiction world. Understanding trademarks is a specialty unto itself. Yes, you can get a cursory understanding from the government's website, but this is definitely an area in which you will want legal counsel. If you feel you have something that is trademark-worthy, I strongly suggest contacting an attorney that specializes in intellectual property, including all the various parameters involved. A few basic points about trademarks you might not be aware of, but I have found helpful:

- Trademark rights are created when a word, phrase, symbol, or image is used in commerce in connection with a product or service.

- You can't trademark a title, but if applicable, you can trademark a word, phrase, or image that is used in connection to a series of books.
- Filing an application to register a trademark with the trademark office grants you additional legal rights.

Another form of protecting your intellectual property is to have your own website. Claiming the URL for your name, your book titles, your teaching model, etc. is always a good idea, especially since it's relatively inexpensive. For only $12 a year, you can secure the URL you want (if it's still available). As the internet continues to expand year after year, more and more URLs will become unavailable. In fact, there's an entire industry that exists to purchase URLs of common names, words, and phrases, and then sell them for an often large fee. I've run into this myself and with some of my friends and fellow authors. So if you can grab the URL for your name and your book, do it!

Finally, one of the more overlooked aspects of being an author is joining a professional group. Along your publishing journey, you may have joined various writing or networking groups to learn more about the industry or to hone your craft. This can always be a good idea, as long as you also practice discernment—especially in the writing groups. Once you're a published author with a certain amount of sales, or when you have an offer for publishing from a publishing house, you will want to look into joining a professional organization, such as the Authors Guild. The Authors Guild is the preeminent organization for published authors.

Organizations like this advocate for the groups they represent (think: AARP). The organization's goal is to protect the best interests of their members, but they also have a lot of resources available that many people don't realize. For example, the Authors Guild has resources to help with legal issues and creating an author's website, to name two. Though there is often an annual membership fee and requirement for joining, a professional group can be very helpful to you in your life as an author. Plus, it's a great way to invest in yourself as a professional.

Beyond these aspects of publishing, there are other professional factors worth considering when addressing where and how you should invest in yourself and your work. Specifically, we're talking about editing and marketing.

Editing

We previously touched on the importance of investing in your work by working with a designer and having it edited. Now we can break down the focus on editing a bit further and look at it by publishing type.

If you're working with a traditional publishing company, they will do the editing for you, but this does not mean that you should submit an unedited manuscript—quite the opposite. In fact, most publishers won't accept a manuscript that isn't clean. Any manuscript you submit anywhere for publication should be edited at least four times, in this order:

- Once by you
- Once by a professional
- Once by a trusted friend/colleague/family member
- Once (again) by you

With the availability of programs and software to improve your written work, there is literally no excuse for submitting a manuscript with errors. Just don't do it. Having other people's eyes on your work helps, too.

Beyond that, there are different types of editing that you should be aware of. Though there is industry-specific lingo for these different types, I have found that it varies based on who I am talking to. So, to make it simpler, I've listed the types based on what they basically do:

- Developmental editing
- Content editing
- Copy editing
- Proofreading

They seem self-explanatory, right? Each type of editing has a specific focus to help create the best book possible. For example, content editing might look at the plot and plot lines and make sure that everything makes sense. After all, if Mr. Chips is going to kill someone with the poison in his pocket, you need to be sure that the poison is there and not a knife. Authors often change details as they are writing because the story evolves. Conducting a good content edit will help clean up errors like these. With each editing pass, you should be cleaning up any issues, including: mistakes, passive voice, clarity, accessibility, etc.

There are free/inexpensive tools like Grammarly that help strengthen your writing as you go that include this kind of evaluation. Are you using too much passive voice? Do you consistently use a common phrase inaccurately? By having a program teach you as you go, you become a better writer. On more than one occasion, I have had good writers say to me, "Well, that was a humbling experience," after they downloaded and turned on Grammarly. We all have blind spots in our writing. We all need editors. If you're self-publishing, there are freelancers and editing companies that specialize in providing just the editing services. If you're not self-publishing but want to become a better writer, invest in yourself and hire a professional editor to help you hone your craft. You will be glad you did.

Speaking of honing your craft, did you know that the "age" of your writing matters? According to the Literacy Project, the average American reads at a 7th/8th grade level.[10] Though it may fluctuate based on genre, most consumer-based books need to be written at this grade level to be most successful. Understanding what grade level is best for your specific book requires doing a bit of research into the genre and then learning where your book lands. To do this, you can use services such as the Flesch-Kincaid readability scale.[11] Some of these services are free, some have a fee. Knowing your readability score in advance of submitting anything is always a good idea. It may also be a requirement of an agent for your book proposal.

If you have been signed by a publishing house, once the traditional publisher has your clean manuscript, they will give it to their editorial department to work with you on improving it. These are experts who you should allow to do their job. Of course, if you feel they are changing your work too much or altering your unique voice, you shouldn't remain silent. Ask them why they're making changes and work with them to achieve the best end result. Again, I think collaboration makes the best product.

Unfortunately, I know too many authors who have taken the editing process personally. I get it. I did that, too, in the beginning. Your book is your baby. It's part of you. Watching someone else make changes can be hard to take. Communication is key at this point, as well as understanding that you are on the same team. Your editor wants you to have success just as much as you do. A healthy

---

10 Marchand, L. (2016, October). What is readability and why should content editors care about it? Center for Plain Language. https://centerforplainlanguage. org/what-is-readability/

11 Good Calculators. (n.d.). Flesh Kincaid calculator. https://goodcalculators. com/flesch-kincaid-calculator/

working relationship with an editor at a traditional publishing company is worth all the time it may take to develop and nurture your work, even if it delays the release date for your book a little bit.

Editing at a hybrid publisher is a bit of a different story. Often this is less about the relationship and more about the service. You are paying for it, after all. Unfortunately, most editing services involved in a hybrid publishing agreement are limited. This means that the typical "back and forth" of a good editing relationship is unavailable, unless you're willing to pay a lot of extra money. Each time more changes are made beyond the scope of the original agreement, there is a fee. You are literally paying "à la carte" for your editor's time. Yet another reason why it's important to do the majority of your editing up front and before submission.

If you're self-publishing, we've already discussed the importance of working with professional editors. The four passes of editing I've previously mentioned will most likely expand to 5–8 or more, depending. Don't skimp on this. If your book is difficult to read or requires the reader to look past simple mistakes, they won't review it well, and you will lose potential readers. This is low-hanging fruit with an easy fix. Don't limit your chances for success before your book is even published. Invest in good editing. You'll be glad you did.

Marketing

Speaking of success, another area where it will pay to invest in your work and yourself as an author is marketing. I've already briefly discussed the love-hate relationship most authors have with marketing. It's a dreaded word, I know. It's rare to find an author that wants to do the business side of getting their work into the world. But in today's publishing game, it's increasingly obvious that without marketing, books don't get seen or read. The biggest tragedy I know of in publishing is learning that someone's beautiful book has never been picked up by anyone. As we discussed previously, marketing doesn't have to be the Mt. Everest you may think it is. Let's go back to the basics once again. To begin with, all marketing is about relationships, and the simple truth is:

Readers don't buy books from publishers.

Readers buy books from people.

Think about it for a moment. Most of the books you've ever bought in your life were because they were recommended to you by a friend, you stumbled on them at a trusted retailer, or you already know of and/or like the author or genre (or another author in the same genre recommended them). Yes, we now have "influencers" on social media where authors can pay to have their books recommended and reviewed. So, there's that. But on the whole, books are bought because of a relationship a reader has with someone in their life.

This doesn't change whether you're at a big traditional publishing company, a hybrid company, or self-published. This is true across the board. A few years ago, I attended a webinar on marketing for authors that the Authors Guild hosted. On the panel, there were two women from the marketing departments at big traditional houses. Here's (paraphrased) what one of the marketing professionals said:

We will often create a list of people that we want to get an advance copy of the book to in order to get a review. We will share this list with the author. Inevitably, when we reach out to the people on this list, we never get a response. When the author does, they are more likely to get a response, usually from about 10–20% of the list.

That's eye-opening, isn't it? The statistics in publishing are not great, when you start to really scratch beneath the surface. Actually, if you're an author, and you haven't taken the time to educate yourself about the industry—especially average book sales and quantity of books published annually—please do yourself a favor and put that at the top of your to-do list.[12] It's not meant to discourage you from fulfilling your dream, it's meant to encourage you to be realistic and understand that being an author is a lifetime commitment. Your book, once published, lives forever. This means that you will forever need to be marketing it in some way. Even if it's just to acknowledge it exists at some point in the future.

Marketing and publishing go hand in hand. It's actually the same for any product-based industry, but especially the consumer-based ones. As a former retail buyer, I know all too well what can happen when something goes viral, as well as what can happen when trends and fads change. Marketing is what helps you to understand the ebbs and flows and how you can navigate them better. Of course, you can outsource this, but you will never be completely absent from it.

If you want to see an example of this, you can do an exercise I have asked my authors to do: Go onto any social media platform and look up a favorite author. If you don't know which platform to pick, I usually use Instagram. Then look up their publisher. Look at their respective accounts and compare how often the publisher mentions that specific author's work vs. how often the author does. One of the examples I have used in the past is world-renowned author Paulo Coelho. If you follow him online, you know that he regularly promotes or mentions his work, even if it's over 30 years old. And frankly, he should. As authors, we all should.

---

12 Some sites you can look at, include: WordsRated.com, IbisWorld.com, Publishers.org, PublishersWeekly.com, InternationalPublishers.org.

I believe that if you're proud of what you've created, it sends the wrong message if you're not willing to share it. If you love what you've written, why wouldn't you want to tell the world, talk about it more, and invite others to experience it? That's marketing. Connecting, sharing, and inviting others to engage with your work is marketing.

This is about building relationships and engaging with your audience. As an author, regardless of how you're published, it's part of your work, your process, and your journey. If you don't want to do it at all—if you don't want to talk about and share your work— you may want to rethink whether you want to be a published author. There is no right or wrong answer here, there's only what's right for you. If writing is your passion, and you're not interested in doing what it takes to be a published author, then writing is enough. I know people like this. They love the craft for the craft's sake. It's beautiful. Plus, if they want to print out their work and share it with a small circle of friends—or just create a copy for themselves— there are ways for them to do that.

If, however, you want to be a published author, then understanding where, when, and how to invest in your work is important. In fact, knowing that you need to invest in your work—and yourself as an author—is key. Some of the best things I can suggest to you, if you're just getting started, are to invest in the following:

- **Hone your craft.** Improve your writing skills and get clear on your style and voice. Practice, practice, practice. Write anything and everything. It doesn't have to be monetized or shared. Just write. Hone your craft to find your voice, and then hone it further.

- **Identify trusted colleagues.** I haven't published anything without running it by others first. Whether it's a full-length book, copy for a website, articles and biographies, or anything else I've done, I always "beta test" it with trusted individuals first (especially my books). Sometimes this has led to my not sharing something publicly, and sometimes it has led to not editing further. Knowing *who* your trusted colleagues are, based on the project, is what's important here. They should know writing and they should know you. These are not proofreaders (you can hire those). These are the people who will be honest with you and help make you a better writer.

- **Discover resources.** There are so many resources available to writers these days, it's sometimes overwhelming. Of course, there are also a lot of scams and empty promises advertised online, so you need to do your due diligence. Knowing what resources exist to help support you in your career can only help you on your journey. The safest place to start is with anything free so that you can learn how to discern between what's worthwhile and what's not. Then, you can invest in those products or services that are more meaningful. Trust me, as someone that has spent way too much money and time on programs that talk a big talk and underdeliver, it's worth finding good resources. (Hint: They're often the ones that are less flashy and don't overpromise.)

Publishing my work and being an author is one of the most rewarding things I've ever done. It never gets old to hear a reader tell me that something I wrote helped them in some way. It's a gift I get to give to others that gives back to me. Publishing other authors' work and getting to witness them experience the same is equally as exciting.

Being a writer is a gift. Being an author is a gift. Whatever you choose to do with your writing career, I hope you enjoy the gift that it is—or can be. And above all else, I hope you want to invest more in yourself and your work.

Writing as a Hobby v. a Career

If you haven't figured it out already, I love writing. I think it's an amazing art form to express yourself, to learn, to experience, and to evolve. It seems that writing never dies. We can still read things that were written thousands of years ago in all different kinds of ways from hieroglyphs to scripts. That's pretty amazing.

It's also amazing that writing seems to be infinite. Ideas are only limited by the quantity of writers writing. Two writers can take the same idea and come up with something different. How cool is that?

Furthermore, writing is something that we all use every day. It doesn't matter if you read books or not—every single day you are confronted with some form of writing. Street signs, stores, transportation, advertising, it's all a form of writing. Someone somewhere had to write what you're seeing or reading—whether they called themselves a writer or not. I read something interesting recently in a weekly newsletter I receive. Dr. Karan Rajan is a surgeon in the U.K. who shares his thoughts every week, and it's always fascinating. In this particular newsletter, he shared a crazy fact: If you read one book a day from age 10 to

80, you will have read over 25,000 books. Considering that millions of books are published each year, there's no way any one person could read even a fraction of what's been written. And yet we still write, we still read, and we still collect books—even if we don't get around to reading them.

Writing is about more than just the words on a page, though. It's about ideas, imagination, and inspiration. It's about humanity processing what it means to be human at any given moment in time. Writing can divide just as it can unite. It can break us down just as it can build us up. Being a writer is truly amazing.

Over the course of my career, I have been lucky enough to write professionally in many different ways. I have taken on tiny copywriting gigs and large ghostwriting projects. From writing full-length books to short biographies, everything I have written has told a story. I have written copy for products, such as wine labels, as well as re-imagined all of the copy for entire websites. Under my own name, I have crossed over genres and written children's books, self-help books, and poetry, with fiction in the works. Writing allows me to explore my own life and mind in ways nothing else can. It has also allowed me to help other writers tell their stories.

I never thought I would be a writer. I didn't seek it out. Writing found me. For that, I am forever grateful. I could have kept it as a hobby, but life had other plans for me. Perhaps the same is true for you.

Knowing how you feel about writing and what it brings to your life can help you navigate the journey to being an author. Understanding that your relationship with writing will change and evolve over time will allow you to be flexible in how you go about pursuing your craft. So let's talk about writing as a hobby vs. writing as a career.

To start with, all writing is a craft. Whether you're a technical writer for a company or a creative copywriter for a brand or blog, all writing is a craft. You are literally making something out of nothing using only raw materials. You are crafting something with words. (This is why one of my previous books is titled *Crafting the Perfect College Essay*, not "writing" the perfect college essay.) As a writer, you are crafting. What you choose to do with that is up to you.

If you want to keep writing as a hobby, there are numerous ways you can share your work with others without layering on the added aspects of business and monetization. You can maintain a blog, you can create a newsletter, or you can keep a journal if you don't want to share anything with others. Writing is still writing, even if it's not shared. (I want to reiterate something here that I said earlier: If you *do* keep a journal, you might want to make provisions for what happens to it if something happens to you. It's just a thought, but if you have things you want to remain private, having a plan for disposal is important.)

Writing for writing's sake—or your own sake—can be highly therapeutic and creative. Your writing is yours to do with as you please, including doing nothing with it. That's one of the beautiful things about writing—you can do it anywhere and do nothing with it. It requires nothing of you, except to show up. You can write with a pen on paper or you can write on a keyboard. Heck, I've often written entire pieces by dictating while I am driving! Writing as a hobby is something you should keep doing even if you end up writing as a career. It will help keep your writing voice supple and flexible while also helping it grow and evolve.

If, however, you want to earn a living from writing and your ultimate goal is to be a published author, then there are some things you need to consider along the way.

1. **Writing professionally is incredibly wide and varied.** The more you limit yourself to one type of writing—or one type of income from your writing—the harder your journey will be. Again, go back and look at the publishing industry statistics if you haven't already. Educate yourself on what's possible with books when it comes to income.

2. **Writing takes many forms.** Just as there are numerous book genres, there are many different forms of writing. For example, there's technical writing and copywriting, among many others. You can create an entire career as a technical writer, if you want. I know people who have done this. Ultimately, however, most writing falls into two categories: a) short-format writing and b) long-format writing.

3. **Writing opportunities are everywhere—and also hard to find.** This is the double-edged sword of writing as a career. Writing is everywhere, so presumably writing opportunities should also be everywhere, and they are. But as authors we often gravitate to the same spaces, which creates a massive amount of competition and limits our access. If you want to write more and get paid for it, you have to broaden your field of inquiry.

4. **Writing for hire is not settling.** There are sites (like Fiverr) where you can list your services for hire. As a writer, especially an aspiring author, it can sometimes feel like taking writing jobs is settling. It's not. Anything that helps you pay your bills while you pursue your writing career and passion to be an author is a positive step on the author's journey. Remember, all writing will only help you hone your craft.

In my own career, here are just a few of the topics I've been paid to write about (in alphabetical order):

Accounting	Infographics
Biographies	Medicine
Cannabis	Moving
Celebrity	Poetry
Children	Products
Cooking	Psychology
Decorating	Social media
Education	Spirituality
Healthcare	Wellness
Hospitality	Wine

The list goes on, but you get the idea. The shortest thing I've ever been paid to write was less than 20 words. The longest have been full-length books I've written as a ghostwriter. I've also written newsletters, advertisements, articles, customer letters, comic strips, social media posts, and formal invitations, to name a few. I've created entire personalities and voices for writing clients from scratch, just as I have also learned how to convert a client's voice into the written word.

Now that you have some idea of what's possible, what are you going to do? Do you want to keep writing as a hobby, or do you want to be a published author? Do you want a career as a writer? Do you want to hone your craft? Do you want to expand your writing world in meaningful ways? Have you learned that there are key elements to being an author that can help you understand and navigate publishing? And most of all, do you understand that the author's journey is as varied as there are writers in the world? I hope so.

Mostly, though, I hope you keep writing.

"Secret" for Success

By now, you've learned that there is no magic formula to being an author, but there are components that are true for everybody, whether you are a Type 1, Type 2, or Type 3 Author. Being an author means taking an idea and building something with words—from scratch—to convey it. An author is an artist who uses language as their medium.

In my opinion, an author is a magician.

We create magic using letters in ways not previously seen. Even with limited alphabets, there is virtually an infinite amount of possibility for how those letters can be arranged. Amazing.

So what does it mean to be "successful" as an author?

Well, to start with, it depends on how you define success. If, for example, your version of success as an author involves mentioning *Harry Potter*, you might be in for disappointment. If, however, your version of success involves hearing from a reader about how your words have impacted them, then you're probably going to have a great career as an author. It may not always be easy, but it will be rewarding.

To have success as an author, there is no magic bullet. There is, however, a formula you can use to increase your chances for success... and it's not a secret. In order to have a successful book, you will need the following:

Good, clean writing
+ A compelling idea
+ Willingness to share your work
+ A plan to share your work

= Successful book!

Again, I encourage you to look at statistics for the publishing industry. While they may seem to be a moving target (and there is a significant lack of transparency in the industry), there are some basics that seem to hold true. I suggest you do this because I *didn't*. When I released my first book, I was incredibly disappointed with how it did until I spoke with a friend who worked in the industry and she told me the statistics.

Once I learned what the average sales were for a "no-name" new author, I quickly realized that I had achieved more than most, especially with a self-published book. Was I able to retire? No. (I wouldn't want to, anyway.) Did I recoup the investments I made in publishing it properly and professionally? Yes, eventually. Like many new authors, I didn't know enough to ask the right questions, so I overspent on certain services. But ultimately, yes, my first book (*What if..?*) made back everything I invested in it and more, in time. In fact, that's what most publishers count on: time.

Over time, every book published *should* make back their original investment. Yes, even the books for which publishers shell out multi-million dollar advances. As I mentioned at the start of this book, even Prince Harry's *Spare* didn't make back the initial advance on its release as many had hoped (or believed) it would. It will take time for it to break even. Whether that's one month or one year, we won't know. But most books, if not the majority of all books, take time to reach their sales potential.

This is why you have to be willing to talk about your book forever. I'll reference Paulo Coelho again here. Coelho still talks about *The Alchemist* regularly even though it's been out for decades. Is it because it's a world-renowned bestseller? Maybe. But he also talks about other books he's written, whether they are bestsellers or not. Whether they are a year old or 10 years old.

In the same way that a parent will talk about their child for their entire life, you should want to talk about your "book baby" for the rest of yours. After all, it's your creation—your unique offering. If *you're* not going to talk about it, why would anybody else?

Your talent for ideas and creating stories will always be unique to you, but developing your talent as a writer alongside a desire to talk about your work is something you can cultivate. A good and compelling story is a requirement, but it's not enough if you want to be successful.

Ultimately, the secret to success as an author comes down to three things combined with how you actually define "success." They are:

- Understanding what type of author you are,
- Identifying what method of publishing is most aligned with you as an author and/or your project, and
- Knowing what you're willing to do to nurture your work and your career.

Whether you choose to write as a hobby or as a career, I hope you have learned what matters to you through this process of exploration and understanding as we consider the different aspects of publishing and what it means to be an author.

A career in writing is possible, even if you're not interested in making the journey as an author. However, I would also suggest that expanding your focus to writing as a career will ultimately make you a better author—and make your author's journey more rewarding. The more experience you get, the more you will be able to hone your craft and improve your writing skills.

Whatever you choose, I hope you keep on writing, and I hope you find new ways to embrace your craft that excite you and feed your writer's soul. I wish you only the best, and I hope all your writing dreams come true.

Author's Note

I recently co-presented a workshop on the basics of how to create a children's book. During the workshop, I received a lot of questions about publishing in general, and I ended up sharing a really short summary of what you have now read in this book. Toward the end of the workshop, one of the participants asked a rather blunt but important question: *Why would anyone want to do anything other than self-publish?* This is the equivalent of: *What's the benefit of going with a publisher?*

Most people who ask these questions are primarily thinking about royalties. In fact, I have found that that's the predominant focus of most authors. Understandably. But if your focus is only on the royalties, you're missing the bigger picture (and you may need to re-read this book).

These types of questions are actually why I wrote this book, so that every writer and aspiring author can know how to answer them for themselves. From my perspective as both an author and a publisher, there is a good answer that addresses both of these questions. Basically, my reply went something like this:

Because most people don't understand or realize all the work a publisher actually does. It's so much more than just editing or book design. Additionally, self-published authors can end up spending a lot of money reinventing the wheel, so to speak, when they try to do things themselves. For example, if my publishing company offers you a contract, you not only get my expertise, but you also get all of the experts that I bring to the table. Plus, with a traditional publisher, you get the backing of the publishing house forever. That's not something small, when you actually think about it.

This gave the participants pause, and most of them nodded in agreement. I went on to share the story of how one of our authors had their work stolen by a third party and listed for sale on Amazon in a different format. We were able to stop the sale of the work and prevent the third party from doing it again because this was part of our publishing agreement. The author was incredibly grateful and said to me, "If we had self-published, I'm not sure we would have even known where to begin, or would have gotten the same results." Because they signed with a publishing house, they didn't have to worry about this now, or in the future.

When you self-publish, you receive everything (aka: all of the royalties) and are responsible for everything (aka: all of the tasks and problems that can arise). Forever. Being self-published is not easy, which is probably why so many people choose hybrid publishing. It's very attractive to be able to just pay someone else to do all the work. I get it. Where I think hybrid publishing falls apart is with the rights and royalties. Many authors often (wrongly) assume they get to keep their rights and royalties when they use a hybrid publisher. As such, it's extra important to read the fine print and really understand what it is you're signing, whether it's with a traditional or a hybrid publisher.

Ultimately though, everything starts with understanding what type of author you are. When you understand what type of author you are and learn the different types of publishing, you can be more deliberate in your efforts to try and achieve the result you want.

Publishing is about a lot more than a percentage of sales. Publishing is a labor-intensive, long process. It's also a labor of love. Books live on forever, which means that they are also a job that needs to be managed forever. When you understand that, it can change your perspective and help you better navigate your journey to becoming—or being—an author.

Exercises and Top Tips

This section is designed to help you get clear on everything you just read and how it applies to you, specifically, and/or your project. Knowing what type of author you are as well as what type of publishing model you prefer is key to experiencing success as an author. Answer the questions in the exercises below and review the Top Tips I've provided to help you better navigate the path to publishing. As always, I wish you all the best in your author's journey!

EXERCISES

For your convenience, the exercises from previous chapters are repeated here and adjusted to be more interactive for you. As always, I believe in taking the time to invest in yourself, so don't rush through these questions. They're designed to make you think and reflect to arrive at the best answer that's true for you. There is no "right" or "wrong" answer. Plus, as I mentioned a few times in the book, your answers can change based on the project you're working on. So in order to get the most out of these exercises, only focus on one project when you answer everything. Allow yourself to get clear by working through these questions.

Exercise #1: Identify What Writing Means to You

Answer these questions on a separate piece of paper or in your favorite journal:

- Why are you a writer?
- What do you love about writing?
- What do you find frustrating about writing?
- What does being an "author" mean to you?

Exercise #2: Knowing Your "Why"

Answer these questions on a separate piece of paper or in your favorite journal:

- What published authors do you look up to, and why?
- What authors do you think poorly of, and why?
- What is your favorite genre to read, and why?
- What genre do you like the least, and why?
- If you had to choose a medium other than writing through which to share your creative ideas, what would it be, and why?
- Who do you want to read your work? Who is your ideal audience?
- Would you still write if nobody ever read it? Why or why not?

Exercise #3: Understanding the Type 1 Author

The Type 1 Author leans more toward wanting to be called a "published author" than wanting to market and share/promote their work. On a scale of 1 to 10, how much do you agree with each of these statements? (0=Disagree, 10=Agree)

Statement	0 — 10
I want to be celebrated for my work.	
I want to be acknowledged for my unique voice.	
I want to reach and connect with my readers.	
I want to earn passive income.	
I want to be a "bestselling" author.	
I do not want to have to do marketing to have my work seen.	
I do not want to maintain a platform to promote my work.	
I do not want to have to focus on sales to reach my audience.	
I do not want to rely on book sales as my sole income.	
I don't like seeing my work as a commercial commodity.	
TOTAL	

Exercise #4: Understanding the Type 2 Author

The Type 2 Author leans more toward wanting to share and promote their volume of work. On a scale of 1 to 10, how much do you agree with each of these statements? (0=Disagree, 10=Agree)

Statement	0 — 10
I want to share my work with the world.	
I want to create and have a platform for my unique voice.	
I want to reach my ideal audience and build connections.	
I want to earn primary income from my book(s).	
I want to be part of the process of sharing my work with the world.	
I want to manage the platform to promote my work.	
I want to engage with my audience in meaningful ways, regularly.	
I want to create change for myself and others.	
I want to positively impact the world with my work.	
I don't place importance on "bestselling" or other awards.	
TOTAL	

Exercise #5: Understanding the Type 3 Author

The Type 3 Author writes for writing's sake. On a scale of 1 to 10, how much do you agree with each of these statements? (0=Disagree, 10=Agree)

Statement	0 — 10
I want to write, regardless of being published.	
I may want to share my work with a select group of people.	
I would write whether anyone ever read it or not.	
I know that writing is my passion, and I prefer it to be a hobby.	
I protect my writing time and find comfort in being able to create.	
I more identify as a "writer" than an "author."	
I enjoy being part of the writing community, in various ways.	
I prefer to write in a genre or theme that's already established.	
I don't want or need to earn an income from my work.	
I love sharing my creative ideas with others for feedback.	
TOTAL	

Now, look at your totals for each author type in Exercises 3-5. The highest number is where you currently most align as an author. You can revisit these exercises based on specific projects, too.

Exercise #6: Understanding Platforms

If you're an author who wants your work to both engage your audience and support you financially, then you will need to engage with your audience, too. In order to do that most effectively, you need to be able to answer these questions:

- What platform does your audience use the most?
- What platform are you most comfortable using, both as an author and as a reader?
- What platform supports the style of engagement you prefer?
- What platform can you commit to using regularly?
- What platforms talk to each other so you can leverage your content?

Exercise #7: Understanding Yourself as an Author

Your books are an extension of you. Understanding that you and your work go together, these questions can help you refine your understanding of what type of writer and author you are in general:

- How does being an author support your goals as a writer?
- What is most meaningful about writing?
- What do you wish you could let go of in the writing process?
- What does it mean to be an "author" in today's world?
- What authors do you want to emulate? Why?
- Where do you most like to find your next book recommendation?
- How else do you share your creative ideas? Why?

Exercise #8: Identifying Which Publishing Model Is Right for You

In order to assess which type of publishing you prefer, answer these questions:
- Why do you want to be published?
- What is the desired outcome you want to achieve with your book?
- What is your budget for bringing your book to life, if you need to make a financial investment?
- How much work are you willing to do?
- What are you willing to give up, and what do you want to retain?
- How quickly do you want to be published?

Exercise #9: Pulling It All Together

Ultimately, the secret to success as an author comes down to three things combined with how you actually define "success"—answer these questions:
- Now that you've read this book, what type of author are you?
- What method of publishing is most aligned with you as an author and/or your project?
- What are you willing to do to nurture your work and your career?
- Many authors define success differently. For some, it's getting a publishing contract or being a "bestselling" author. For others, it's about connecting with their audience and gaining a loyal following of readers, and anything in between. So how do you define "success" as an author? Has your

definition changed now that you've gained a deeper understanding of publishing?

Whether you choose to write as a hobby or as a career, I hope you have learned what matters to you through this process of exploration and understanding as we consider the different aspects of publishing and what it means to be an author.

Ten Top Tips

Writing can be a lonely process, but publishing can feel like a veritable quagmire. Here are ten Top Tips you can use to help you navigate the publishing world with greater ease:

1. Do your homework. Research the agents, publishing companies, and/or imprints you are interested in based on your genre.
2. Consider the amount of time for the other things that go into publishing a book beyond writing and editing, such as: designing a cover that fits in the genre but is still unique, marketing (especially if you're a Type 2 Author), copyrights, negotiating royalties and prices, formatting, etc.
3. The best way for people to hear about your book is for you to talk about it.
4. Really make use of all the free information that is available to help you be a better writer and to navigate the publishing industry better.
5. Accessibility is a key factor in having a good book. Use different tools to help you make your work more accessible. For example, if you're writing a nonfiction book, subheads help divide the categories to make it easier for readers.
6. If you're a fiction writer, limit your use of passive voice.

7. If you're writing a children's book, remember to plan for the words on the page to take up more space than you think. Artists like to fill up blank space, but don't forget that the words will take up a lot of room.

8. Reading your writing out loud will help you catch mistakes in general, but it's even more important for children's books. Children's books—especially rhyming ones—have a sing-song quality about them, as they are mostly read aloud. Therefore, the cadence and rhythm of the words matter. If you stumble when reading it aloud, something needs to change.

9. When editing your own work, use an app like Grammarly and learn where you make the same consistent mistakes to improve your writing.

10. Remember to have multiple people read your drafts. Different people and different perspectives will help you see things better.

Resources

Just as with everything else, the internet can be a great source of information and inspiration. It can also be a minefield of disinformation and people taking advantage of others. In order to assist you with your author's journey, here are a few sites I would recommend today, in 2023. Of course, please do your own due diligence. Ask questions, seek referrals and recommendations from friends and colleagues. Don't take anything at face value without scratching a bit beneath the surface. An informed consumer makes better—and smarter—decisions.

The Authors Guild — I referred to them a few times in the book. They are a great resource for existing and aspiring authors alike. www.authorsguild.org

Women in Publishing Summit — A great resource for authors and publishers alike. www.womeninpublishingsummit.com

Publisher's Weekly — The trade publication for the publishing world. A digital subscription is a good value and investment in your career. www.publishersweekly.com/

Writer's Digest — Another trade publication that does its best to support writers and authors with valuable information and vetted resources. www.writersdigest.com

Kirkus Reviews — One of the most trusted and established publishing industry companies. www.kirkusreviews.com

Library of Congress/Copyright Office — www.copyright.gov

Bowker Identifier Services — Link to purchase ISBNs and barcodes: www.myidentifiers.com or to learn more about ISBNs: www.bowker.com

Acknowledgments

As with everything I write, there is always a team of wonderful and talented people supporting me. I couldn't do what I do without you, and I thank you: Franny, Lisa, Michelle & Joe, and Myra. Additionally, I send a special thank you to Teri and Julianne for being early readers of *The Author's Journey*. Your suggestions were incredibly valuable, and I appreciate your time and contribution to making the final manuscript even better. To Winter, my go-to editor, thank you for always having my back, double-checking my work, and cleaning up my excessive comma usage! I'd also like to thank my interns, Katherine and Jordan, for helping me clarify some of my ideas as you learned more about the publishing and editing process. I think internships are a great way to learn, and I value my interns' contributions. I've been lucky to have some of the best!

About the Author

Martina E. Faulkner has been a professional writer for almost two decades, with clients from decorators and designers to wellness professionals and fellow authors. Her extensive portfolio of writing ranges from full-length books to brief bios, and almost everything in between. Whether it's creating wine labels for a vineyard, ghostwriting a groundbreaking book for a doctor, imagining a memoir with a fictitious character, or exploring life in her own words, writing is Martina's creative vehicle of choice.

In 2015, she started her first publishing company with her book *What if..?* She was then inspired to help other authors share their unique voices with the world, and the company grew to become what it is today. Inspirebytes Omni Media (IOM) has allowed Martina to work with countless writers as she helps them make their dream of becoming an author a reality. With everything from memoirs to children's books, non-fiction to poetry, and fiction to cookbooks and photography books, IOM allows Martina to apply her extensive expertise as both a writer and certified coach to the process of publishing. With almost a decade of experience in the ever-changing publishing industry, Martina knows how to help guide writers to create their best book, making the process easier... and more enjoyable!

Learn more at MartinaFaulkner.com

OTHER WORK BY THE AUTHOR

50 and F*ck It!

What if..?

Infinite In My Heart

Crafting the Perfect College Essay

The College Essay Workbook

CHILDREN'S BOOKS AS TIA MARTINA

When the World Went Quiet

Princess Wigglebottom and the Forgotten Christmas

UPCOMING RELEASES

I Am Not ____ Enough (Late 2023)

Me: 365 — A 5-Year Question-A-Day Journal (Late 2023)

The 50 and F*ck It! Workbook (Late 2023)

I Love You More Than the Universe (2024)

Being Human Is Hard (2024)

Client Sessions: Volume 1 (2025)